Praises for *Practice Law Like an Ironman:*

Steve Adams started out as an Assistant Hamilton County Prosecutor
and took his Great American Dream of starting, creating, and building
his own solo practice. His dream came true, and he has one of the best solo
practices in the Midwest. This book is an indispensable resource to
any other lawyer who wants to pursue their Great American Dream
of having a thriving solo practice or small firm.

– BILL CUNNINGHAM, 700 WLW Radio talk show host
and the host of *The Bill Cunningham Show*

I suggest this is a must-read for *all* attorneys, not just solo practitioners.
At the core of any legal practice, and at each impact of the legal system, are
people. Staying focused on people dynamics and how they connect to every part
of building a legal practice is hard work that requires constant attention and
full commitment. Steve's strategy will resonate with anyone interested in getting
better at it—even those of us who never will see a real Ironman course.

– JILL P. MEYER, Lawyer and President/CEO
of the Cincinnati USA Regional Chamber of Commerce

Starting a law firm is overwhelming, and it is difficult to find great advice on how
to do it successfully. *Practice Law Like an Ironman* fills that void with actionable
systems and checklists that tell you exactly what to do, while also showing you
how to develop the much needed entrepreneurial mindset you need.
If you are starting your law practice, this book is essential.

– JOLEENA LOUIS, Esq, Joleena Louis Law

Steven R. Adams is one of the nation's leading DUI/criminal defense attorneys, a sought-after public speaker and author with a thriving solo practice based in Cincinnati, Ohio.

Named one of Ohio's Top 100 lawyers, Adams has established himself as a master of marketing. In *Practice Law Like an Ironman*, he offers a unique workshop program for any lawyer aspiring to build a solo or small practice of their own. His versatile strategy employs an unbeatable marketing master plan, and an office set-up protocol, that can be tailored to any niche of the law.

Over the course of his career, Steve has served as a judicial law clerk, prosecutor and political campaign manager. Not least impressive, he is a four-time Ironman world championship competitor. The Iron Man experience taught Adams motivational principles that have successfully driven him to continually improve and become the best in law—and life.

Practicing Law Like An Ironman works! Since leaving the DA's office and founding his solo practice 16 years ago, Steve has more than quadrupled his income, all while building a large national following, and appearing on a host of radio and TV programs.

PRACTICE LAW LIKE AN
IRONMAN

Unbeatable Checklists
for any Lawyer Creating and Building a Solo or Small Practice

STEVEN R. ADAMS

Printed in the United States of America.

ISBN Paperback: 978-0-9994166-1-7
ISBN Hardcover: 978-0-9994166-2-4
ISBN eBook: 978-0-9994166-0-0

SRA Legal Enterprises
8 West Ninth Street,
Cincinnati, OH 45202

First Edition, 2017

Cover/Interior Design: Michelle Manley

To my Mom, Sally, and to my late father, Don, both of whom lovingly instilled in me an Ironman work ethic—one that has served me throughout my life..

Acknowledgements

First and foremost, I want to thank my beautiful wife Maria and my two amazing sons, Sam and Abe. I'm eternally grateful for all their love, encouragement, and support as I continue to build my Ironman law practice. When you work as hard as I do, it's a gift to come home to such an incredible family.

I also want to recognize all the coaches, advisors, mentors, and colleagues who have guided me through the various stages of my life and career, not to mention my alma mater, Chase College of Law, and its law professors, where my legal training all began.

A special shout out to Jim Frooman, who was my law school study partner (a great friend who helped me not panic when I cut my head open the early morning hours before the bar exam!).

As far as the production of this book is concerned, a huge thanks to my editor, best-selling author Glenn Plaskin. He is amazing, and his vision, writing, and editorial skills are truly brilliant, second to none! He has become a great friend to me and to my staff.

Next, there's my incredible office team, including my paralegals Jennifer Blum and Tiffany Teuschler (a.k.a. Jen and Juice.) I could not do without you. The amount of work delegated to each of you is substantial, and you never fail to get it right!

Jen, you were a fantastic project manager for this book. And I can never thank you enough for your endless loyalty and devotion. You make us a great team.

Our book designer, Michelle Manley, captured my vision for the graphics and visuals of the Ironman Law Practice, on both the cover and on the interior pages.

To Carrie Hartunian Smith for all of her carefully crafted marketing strategy and advice in launching this book.

On a personal note, thank you to my friend, Judge Scott T. Gusweiler, who connected me to Judge Norbert Nadel. It was Judge Nadel, in turn, who gave me my first legal job ever as his court clerk. While I didn't make much, the experience was priceless—and a great deal of fun.

I'm also thankful to Joseph T. Deters and the late Arthur M. Ney, Jr., who hired me as an Assistant Hamilton County Prosecutor. Those eight years were a tremendous period of training that allowed me to grow as a trial lawyer and to build relationships.

And I'm incredibly grateful to the great Randy Freking and his firm of Freking Myers & Reul, who hired me and gave me the privilege to work in a civil law firm. It was Randy who unselfishly mentored and encouraged me to start my own criminal practice.

A big hug to Bill and Penny Cunningham for their amazing support and friendship. Bill, you catapulted my solo practice to a level beyond what I imagined. Featuring me on your radio show and connecting me with other radio show hosts have been terrific boosts to my practice and a great deal of fun. Bill "Segman" Dennison, thank you as well.

And thanks to:

My mentors and friends Joe Honerlaw, Merlyn Shiverdecker, Scott Croswell, Tom Fisher, Bill Busemeyer, Glenn Whitaker, Steve Tolbert, Ken Stone, and Zach Smith. Your friendship, wisdom and guidance is invaluable.

Also, a big thanks to my Ironman training pals: Troy Jacobson, Eric Hodska, Tom Sicking, Steve Busse, Dan Casey , and Jerry Frentsos. Thank you for your friendship, and also for pushing and challenging me to accomplish my goals.

Tad Brittingham. Your Ironman lawyering skills have served you well, and you have a brilliant career ahead of you.

Jenny Sciortino, for being my social media guru and website developer... an Ironwoman Rock Star!

My law clerks Doug Rebok, Brittany Grigery and Kevin Teran. Your youth, wisdom, and brilliance are greatly appreciated. Also, thank you Jennifer Hedge, lawyer extraordinaire, whose wisdom and brilliance is appreciated as well!

Christina Moore (my former paralegal) who has decided to stay at home and raise her beautiful family. Your work ethic was incredible and you are truly missed around the Law Offices of Steven R. Adams.

My Client Intake Specialist Amy Averett. Your professional, calming, and empathetic qualities have been indispensable to our firm's ability to interface with clients.

Dan Stratford for his invaluable help towards www.notguiltyadams.com and his digital marketing assistance.

My banking buddies who always help me strike the right deal: Jim Uebel, Dave Pierce and Sue Cummings.

My accounting team of Tony and Tonya Mort, and Lizz Rettig for keeping me financially on the law practice Ironman course.

My best friend of many years Mark Ayer, who has given me tremendous advice and counsel, and has helped me learn the "art of the deal." I always appreciate your encouragement and confidence in me.

Mike Blum and Jason Dudas. We live in a video age now. Your videos are Ironman rock solid! Your ability to make the seriousness of law funny, entertaining, and educational all at the same time is a gift.

My clients, lawyer colleagues, and people in the community who refer me business. Without you I wouldn't be where I am today, so thank you so much!

All the authors of the books that I've listed in this book. Without you, I would have nothing to write about, and you guys and gals do a great service to those who want to have Ironman-like businesses.

The judges and lawyers who like me and who don't like me. Together, you make me a better lawyer.

Last, but not least, thank you God! You have blessed me with a great family, a great practice, great friends, and a great life.

TABLE OF CONTENTS

Introduction

"Swim like you're gonna drown, ride like you stole it, and run like they are chasing you."
-Anonymous Ironman competitor who made it to the finish line-

The Ironman Triathlon World Championship is the most treacherous one-day endurance race in the world.

It encompasses a staggering 140 miles from beginning to end. If you're lucky enough to finish it, you never forget the exhilaration and exhaustion of that long day in Kona, Hawaii.

I've done it four times.

It all begins with a 2.4-mile swim, either in the open ocean (as I did it in Hawaii), or in a lake or river. You then jump onto your bike for a 112-mile ride. Finally, you finish the day (hopefully) by running a regulation-length marathon of 26.2 miles.

You have 17 hours to complete the entire feat. My best time was 9 hours and 55 minutes. In the occupational division of participating lawyers, I was the number one lawyer in the world three times.

How did I do it? Crazy preparation! It can't be done in a day, week, or month. You have to set out for a year or more, building up your endurance, practicing multiple miles per week, and visualizing yourself competing and winning. Mental attitude is everything. You have to continually chip away at your fear of any limitation.

It's the same thing in building a solo law practice. I believe you can *Practice Law Like an Ironman.* HOW?

- Set a goal
- Work for it passionately
- Exercise discipline
- Be resilient
- Build a team around you

That's what it takes to cross any finish line in life.

I always say that I may not be the most talented person in the world, but I'll outwork anybody when I put my mind to something. I work smart and hard, and I figure it out from there. Even when I have an injury or setback, I keep grinding away, pushing past it to get to the prize. It's a journey, not an event.

That's why I believe that building a law practice is like preparing for an Ironman race. I had to educate myself to compete. And to do it successfully, I needed a SYSTEM, similar to the systems we're going to talk about in this book.

I also needed a vision statement to define a remarkable goal. That goal became my North Star. It's the same for you. Creating a law practice is a mission, not a hobby. And, of course, you need an iron will to execute the mission.

Sure, it can be painful. At times, you're going to feel afraid, nervous, and anxious. But a powerful action plan will always be your guide to trumping fear.

As I look back on my Ironman experience now, I see so clearly that those 10-hour days of furiously swimming, biking, and running toward the finish line changed me as a man. It affected everything that followed—the life I created with my wife and two sons, the career I built as a lawyer, and the energized spirit I try to bring to my community.

That's why I always say that the lessons of Ironman have driven me throughout my entire life. And even though my last competition was in 2002, I still think of myself as an Ironman—and I try to live like one. I apply Ironman values on a daily basis to create success everywhere I go—at the office, in court, in client meetings, seminars, you name it.

I now offer you the same principles in the pages that follow. You're going into training, beginning the greatest race of your life. And you're going to face stiff competition.

✶ ✶ ✶ ✶ ✶

HERE'S A STARTLING FACT: Did you know that each year American law schools churn out 39,000 newly minted lawyers![1]

Think about it. In a country already overrun with 1.2 million attorneys,[2] this army of law school grads, many of them burdened by student debt, floods the market. And competition has become increasingly brutal.

In fact, since the economic downturn of 2008, the legal sector has lost 54,000[3] jobs. So it's not surprising that only 65 percent[4] of law school

---

1 https://lawschooltuitionbubble.wordpress.com/original-research-updated/law-graduate-overproduction/
2 https://www.bostonglobe.com/opinion/2014/05/09/the-lawyer-bubble-pops-not-moment-too-soon/qAYzQ823qpfi4GQl2OiPZM/story.html
3 https://www.law360.com/florida/articles/126393/legal-industry-jobs-severely-reduced-in-september
4 https://www.bloomberg.com/news/articles/2014-06-20/the-employment-rate-falls-again-for-recent-law-school-graduates

graduates find full-time, long-term employment (one graduate from the Thomas Jefferson School of Law in San Diego even sued her alma mater for fraud after an unsuccessful three-year job search).

What do the *rest* of them do?

With the market so squeezed, some are taking jobs as public defenders, while others find employment in the private sector in jobs that do not even necessarily require bar admission.

But an increasing number of lawyers are breaking out on their own, opening up a solo practice or starting a small firm. If you're in this category, this is the book for you.

The share of recent law graduates going solo increased from 3.5 percent in 2008 to over 7 percent today. And many are thriving—both in terms of income and in terms of personal satisfaction.

In fact, legions of solo practitioners are developing their new practices in a variety of ways. Social media-minded Millennials, for example, may believe that they can successfully create a practice simply by hanging out a virtual shingle. With just a cell phone, a laptop, and a website, they're off and running—or not!

Sure, technology is turning the tide in the practice of law, allowing these kinds of instant start-ups without the need to rent an office, manage a support staff, or create face-to-face social networks.

But as you'll see in the pages ahead, **effectively marketing your business also depends upon live interaction with potential clients and colleagues and building a person-to-person network.** There's nothing that can replace direct human contact, which is why trials are not conducted via telephone or Skype.

So rather than sitting behind a keyboard, to develop your solo practice you need to attend events and conventions, get involved in the community, schedule lunch dates, spend time at the courthouse getting to know people, and explore areas for pro bono contribution. It may be old school, but it works. Hiding behind a computer like a drone is not the answer.

In all these aspects and more, supporting and guiding solo practitioners is the mission of this book, which will demonstrate how to start, manage, and build your business. It's a practical guide covering the myriad issues facing any lawyer who wants to create an autonomous, profitable practice.

REMEMBER: *You're the boss. And everything here is customized to your passions and skill sets.*

Here's what's totally unique about this book…instead of a narrative description of how to get started, you'll find a comprehensive series of *checklists* and *questions* to help you organize the necessary tasks. This allows you to "think in bullet points." You stay focused on a logical sequence of steps to attain each goal.

You'll also find passages of inspirational wisdom and selected stories that illustrate some of my own experiences, all meant to guide you.

It's a lot to digest all at once, but use this guide like a workbook. At any point, you can go to the Table of Contents and skip from section to section as needed. Just pick out an issue related to a specific goal and then follow my recommendations step-by-step. The checklist format cuts right to the chase, without a lot of fluff.

As you'll see, these checklists will assist the lawyer in understanding:

- How to powerfully motivate your team by building transparency, trust, and chemistry.
- How to network and get lucrative referrals.
- What it takes to master social media and digital marketing.
- The principles of law office management.
- The art of handling legal fees and billing.
- The technique of effective delegation.
- How to become a recognized authority in your chosen niche.
- Ethics and professional conduct.

✳ ✳ ✳ ✳ ✳

There is also the human factor, so what follows is a roadmap to not just your business success, but also to your fulfillment as an employer, mentor, and community leader.

To accomplish this, we need to **cultivate a powerful entrepreneurial mindset**—a winning attitude. Many of you who pick up this book are already upbeat, driven, and enterprising, but we can always improve our state of mind, making it even more positive. That's why the opening chapters of this book focus on positive thinking, which is an absolute must for success.

My inspiration is drawn from over 100 books that have motivated me, all of them listed in the reading list at the end of this book. They include such classics as Seth Godin's *Purple Cow*, John Jantsch's *Duct Tape Marketing*, and John C. Maxwell's *Developing the Leader Within You.*

Also, other classics such as *Go-Givers Sell More* (Bob Burg and John David Mann); *Mad Genius: A Manifesto for Entrepreneurs* (Randy Gage); *The E-myth Attorney: Why Most Legal Practices Don't Work and What to Do About It* (Michael Gerber).

I've also drawn from my 25-year law experience, first as an assistant prosecuting attorney in Hamilton County, Ohio, where I tried hundreds of misdemeanor and felony cases over a period of eight years; then as a civil plaintiff attorney at an employment firm (guided by my incredible mentor and boss, Randy Freking, founding partner of Freking Myers & Reul, one of Ohio and Cincinnati's top labor and employment lawyers). Today I am a solo practitioner focused on criminal and DUI defense, having recently added family law.

Before hanging out my own shingle 16 years ago, I wish I had one good guide that would have given me concrete systems for networking, marketing, and making the management of a law office flow efficiently. It would have hugely helped to build the practice and make it more streamlined and productive.

In my solo beginning, I taught myself by using direct mail, radio, and other media. I had many of my systems in my head, but nothing was written out and it was a process of trial and error.

First off, I had to come up with a game plan. I started by mapping out a unique direct mail marketing campaign. I also initiated "Jail Mail" in order to obtain criminal and DUI clients. Essentially, I would go to the sheriff's department every morning between 5:00 and 5:30 am and scour the criminal blotter of those arrested and in jail. I sifted through it and assessed which defendants were likely to have enough resources to hire a lawyer.

I was also fortunate that my mentor Randy Freking leased me a reasonably priced office and conference room, and allowed me use of a secretary from his firm. This had a huge effect.

I went from earning $42,000 a year to $240,000 in my first year going solo. Amazingly, I accomplished this with minimal overhead or the outlay of other business expenditures. And from that point forward, my practice became exponentially more lucrative year after year, with a 2015 gross of over $1 million. You'll see how I did it in the chapters to follow.

As I learned, though, nothing lasts forever. My practice defending DUI defendants has slowly taken a hit with the advent of Uber, Lyft, and other app-accessible or online car services that are now being used by my "ideal" clients. As a result, the defense practice I've relied upon is slowly dying, which has motivated me to initiate a new niche... family law (divorce, dissolutions, pre-nuptial agreements, and adoption).

My own example proves that a law practice is always a work-in-progress, and that shifting trends and markets require fast footwork. This means you have to be prepared for reinvention and regrowth. This book will help you survive those tough times of transition when your client base changes and when you need conflict solutions in or out of the courtroom.

As you'll read, no matter how your business evolves, one of the true secrets to a successful practice is mastering people skills—the ability to effectively communicate and to empathize with your colleagues and clients. You eliminate impulsive or aggressive behaviors and interact respectfully to build sincerity and trust.

In the end, life isn't always fair. There will always be a new challenge up ahead, regardless of your legal skills. Lawyers need to deal with "the law practice of life" with the right attitude, which is a test of your ability to be agreeable and flexible. This mindset allows you to get out of a rut and pivot in another direction when you need to. You'll find the key to doing it here.

More than ever, in addition to the right mindset, a solo practitioner needs to master a variety of specific skills. You need to effectively utilize technology and social media, including the use of blogs and digital marketing. You also will want to produce great brochures, newsletters, and even books. Perfecting team-building and people skills, networking astutely, and using appropriate techniques for branding your practice are also vital.

Not to mention the necessity of media promotion. In my case, Cincinnati's top radio talk-show host, Bill Cunningham of 700 WLW, has been a great friend, mentor, and super-charger of my practice. In 2003, I helped him out on a case *pro bono*, and I've appeared on The *Bill Cunningham Show* many times to discuss my landmark cases since then. I can tell you that those interviews with him catapulted my practice to a top-of-the-line presence in southwest Ohio and Northern Kentucky. Not to mention Bill referred me to a woman who allegedly failed to pay a $1.16 in city income tax. Shockingly, she was criminally charged for not paying that paltry amount. I was eventually able to get this crazy case dismissed, and received worldwide media attention.

In short, having media contacts who tout your work is hugely helpful. So wherever you might be, there are local radio, newspaper, and television reporters who will be key to promoting your practice too.

None of these topics, I should add, are adequately, if ever, addressed in law school. Yes, we're drilled in legal theory and in the study of torts, contracts, property law, criminal law, and civil procedure. But not emphasized are the practical business techniques or motivational principles that lawyers must use to enhance both their efficiency and their happiness.

All in all, the greatest challenge to a solo practitioner is managing all the irons in your fire. You have to cope with everything from budgeting and hiring staff to branding, marketing, and customer service, plus the legal work itself—the research, writing, and court dates. Juggling it all isn't easy. It's like having five kids! It's a huge balancing act. This book will be a companion tool for helping you through it all. Let's begin!

PART ONE

YOUR POINT OF VIEW:
The Formula of a Positive Attitude

1. **The Entrepreneurial Leap**

2. **Dancing with Fear**

3. **Transform Your Thinking, Change Your Life**

4. **8 Secrets to a Positive Mindset**
   - Secret #1: Self-Awareness and an Attitude Quiz
   - Secret #2 Affirmations
   - Secret #3 Faith
   - Secret #4 Relaxation
   - Secret #5 Choosing the Right Peer Group
   - Secret #6 The Art of Giving
   - Secret #7 Being Thankful
   - Secret #8 Visualization

1

The Entrepreneurial Leap

"An entrepreneur is someone who jumps off a cliff and builds a plane on the way down."
– Reid Hoffman, Executive Chairman of LinkedIn –

I always think of a true entrepreneur as an adventurer with a huge imagination; someone willing to assume a degree of risk to make a dream become a reality. As a solo practitioner, you become an independent-minded leader with a unique vision that pushes you forward.

What drives you?

It's the power of imagination—the ability to create a vision of your idealized future. You don't bend to the expectations of others. You don't follow the pack. You make it happen. You think outside the box. And you take on the risks for the ultimate prize; personal freedom, financial abundance, and the ability to own your time.

That's the dream.

You don't need me to tell you that entrepreneurship is the pathway to fulfilling your vision. Just watch an episode of Shark Tank. Somebody with an innovative product and an astute marketing plan launches themselves from a conventional life to mogul status.

True, as an independent entrepreneur, you relinquish the security of a 9-to-5 corporate job. In fact, especially at the beginning, as you develop an employer-based mindset, your workday may extend to 12 or 16 hours a day. But it's worth it, because it's your mission. You own it. You're the boss. You're the visionary. And it will be primarily you who earns the benefits of all that hard work.

Any new enterprise, of course, has an element of calculated risk built into it. And often with risk comes fear . . . the sense of being worried or anxious about embarking on something new.

Success can't find you if you're hiding in your comfort zone, so you have to be willing to take a risk.

When I was first establishing myself as a solo practitioner, and feeling nervous about it, I turned to one of my favorite writers, Seth Godin. He's the author of 17 books, including *Tribes: We Need You to Lead Us* and *Linchpin: Are You Indispensable?* Reading his work always reminded me that **FEAR** is the absolute enemy of the entrepreneur.

Godin was able to conquer it—and in a big way.

At age 26, he started a book packaging business with $20,000 in savings—and he's now worth $34 million. **How did he do it?** By being bold and innovative, and by using contests, online games, and scavenger hunts to market companies to participating users. He never yielded to fear.

In one of my all-time favorite books, *Think and Grow Rich*, Napoleon Hill summarized what he viewed as the six basic human fears—poverty, criticism, ill health, loss of love, old age, and death. But there are other fears too. What about the fear of public speaking? Fear of strangers, of terrorist attacks, of intimacy, of loneliness, of failure, of rejection, of commitment, even the fear of spiders? You name it, we fear it.

In business, as in the Ironman competition, fear of failure is a huge liability. And one antidote to it is laser-focusing on your goal. You've got to be like a hockey player with tunnel vision, solely concentrating on the puck, blocking out all the noise and distractions from the crowd, players, and press in order to guard the goal. Without this self-discipline, winning isn't possible.

2
Dancing with Fear

"You must control your mind and make a blanket decision that nothing which life has to offer is worth the price of any fear."
– Napoleon Hill, *Think And Grow Rich* –

What *is* fear?

We all know it pretty well. Right from childhood, it's one of the emotions we dislike most—that dreaded feeling that signals danger, pain, or threat.

It evokes instant unhappiness. When it hits, some people start sweating, others have chest pain, cold flashes, or breathlessness. You feel anxious, sometimes helpless, even alarmed.

THE GOOD NEWS: *Primal fear is a good thing.*

It protects us from immediate dangers or threats. It's healthy because it keeps us safe. And it provokes an adrenaline blast when a call to action is needed. We should be afraid of a rattlesnake, road rage, falling off the edge of a cliff, violent weather, or a physical threat.

But then there are unhealthy fears—the ones that keep us from taking chances or moving forward. One great acronym for FEAR is...

FALSE EVIDENCE APPEARING REAL.[5]

---

5 http://www.awaken.com/2013/01/overcoming-f-e-a-r-false-evidence-appearing-real/s

4

This is when we look for any conceivable thing that could possibly go wrong in the future and project each and every negative possibility.

We think of the What If's:

- *What if this practice doesn't work?*
- *What if the clients don't find me?*
- *What if my competition crushes me?*
- *What if I'm not skilled enough to run my own business?*

This crescendo of false expectations looms over us and blocks out innovation. These what ifs are the antithesis to positive thinking.

* * * * * * *

REMEMBER : *Many of the greatest figures in history found themselves born into modest circumstances or faced with serious personal challenges that led to overwhelming fears. Yet their contribution was immense.*

For Example

- **HENRY FORD** failed five times in various businesses before he founded the Ford Motor Company.

- **R.H. MACY** started seven businesses that all failed before hitting it big with Macy's.

- **BILL GATES** was a college dropout with a failed first business before he created the global giant Microsoft.

- **HELEN KELLER** became deaf and blind before her second birthday.

- **WALT DISNEY** was fired from a newspaper for "lack of imagination," couldn't pay his rent and was surviving on dog food before he hit it big.

- **R. K. ROWLING** was a single mother living on welfare when she wrote the first Harry Potter book.

- **ANDREW CARNEGIE,** at 13, worked in a cotton mill earning $1.20 per week.

- **STEVE JOBS,** given away by his biological parents, was ousted from Apple.

- **ABRAHAM LINCOLN** had multiple failures and setbacks—he was demoted in the army, failed in business, and lost elections to congress before becoming president.

- **DEMOSTHENES,** who stuttered, became the greatest orator in ancient Athens.

- **JULIUS CAESAR** was an epileptic.

- **NAPOLEON** graduated 46th out of 65 at his military academy.

- **BEETHOVEN AND THOMAS EDISON** (after a bout of scarlet fever during childhood) were both deaf.

- **CHARLES DICKENS AND HANDEL** were lame.

- **HOMER** was blind.

- **SIR WALTER SCOTT,** who had polio as a child, was paralyzed in the right leg.

Each of these great figures had what author John C. Maxwell *(Developing the Leader Within You)* calls "an inner fire" that could never be extinguished.

You have it too. And the lesson their lives offer:

It doesn't matter where or how your life begins, what circumstances you're born into, or what adversity you face. Human beings have the capacity to surmount any challenge—poverty, disability, or tragic setback.

In all the examples of famous people we know, one important key to their contribution was **persistence and defiance of fear or limitation.** Each of them failed frequently at first, failing their way to success.

The opposite of success is not failure, but mediocrity. Failure is simply part of the success process. Failures are really just momentary stepping stones to success. From failures you learn great lessons and modify strategies. It teaches you lessons, develops your character, and allows you to modify your approach to find the right way to reach greatness. You also develop the necessary character and resilience to become a seasoned professional.

– RANDY GAGE, *Mad Genius: A Manifesto for Entrepreneurs* –

Shark Tank billionaire, **MARK CUBAN** said that failure is part of the success equation. For example, he once tried selling powdered milk, which he says was a fast lesson in failure.

"I honestly thought it would make a killer business, and it lasted minutes! It doesn't matter how many times you fail. Each time only makes you better, stronger, smarter, and you only have to be right once. Just once! Then everyone calls you an overnight success and you feel lucky. I still feel that way."

So what really is the formula to success?

It often starts with one or more failures, then a success, then more failures after that, followed by a success!

For example, after becoming interested in politics in my 20's, I ran for the Ohio state legislature at age 33. I worked my tail off, created an agenda of issues that were key to my community, and raised a lot of money. But I lost in a primary battle, and wound up very disappointed.

Yet every time I think of it now, I *thank* my opponent. Why? Instead of making $40,000 a year as a state representative, I'm doing much better as a solo practitioner, and I'm actually happier not working in the political climate of today, though I support candidates I like, network with them, and even host fundraisers. But instead of a political focus, I wanted to create my own business.

True, many people shy away from the steep climb of entrepreneurship, and find predictable secure jobs, though they may offer little room for growth or excitement. By refusing to engage risk, you begin to fear movement of any kind. But that's not the route for the solo practitioner. You're making it or striking out on your own. You're using your highly developed skills to create a lucrative practice and beyond.

In my own life, as an offshoot of writing this book, I envision developing a seminar business too, using the principles of what you're reading as a guide for a program geared toward newly-graduated lawyers (and established practitioners too, lawyers already out in the field for 1-10 years), committed to further developing their solo practices.

They would benefit from networking with experts in the field. Great speakers procured for the seminar would share their life experiences and models for success. The participants would also have the chance to network with one another, making alliances that would ultimately further their careers and perspectives.

Toward that end, I recently engaged a marketing firm to create the branding for the seminar side of the business and to handle all its social media, including a website. I also had a meeting with the head of the career development department at my alma mater, the Salmon P. Chase College of Law. She reinforced my belief that the production of this book and the creation of a seminar business were viable ideas. In fact, once all the logistics for the seminar business are in place, she offered to distribute the marketing materials to third-year, graduating law students at Chase. She also provided me a list of

200 career development heads at prominent law schools. Talk about the upside of scheduling a meeting and connecting! Initiating this kind of networking was the key to overcoming my fear of expanding from where I am to where *I want to be.*

There are days, of course, when I feel the stress and pressure of turning a vision into a reality, but you cannot let that uncertainty stop you. That's what dancing with fear is all about—taking one action after another and stomping out negative thoughts. Sure, the business might flounder or even fail at first. But remember, as Seth Godin says,

"The cost of being wrong is less than the cost of doing nothing!"

So how do we eliminate (or reduce) fear?

According to **GODIN,** that's the wrong question. The real issue, he says, is *"How do I dance with fear?"*

"The answer to fear is TAKING ACTION.
For fear is not the enemy—paralysis is."
-Seth Godin-

By this, he means that you have to **use the intense energy fear consumes and turn it into persistence, drive, and discipline.**

Entrepreneurs must learn how to actively talk themselves OUT of fear. You counteract self-doubt by *Acting As If*—taking the right **actions and allowing the results to unfold.**

We have to be willing to step onto the "high wire" so to speak, with an acceptance of risk until we're able to solidify our practice and feel confident in it.

9

Never assume that risk is a bad thing, unless you're unprepared for it. But with the right tools, talents, and careful preparation and planning, risk is really an open-ended invitation for success.

But even when your solo practice is financially successful, there are inevitable stresses and fears that can easily bog you down. Let me give you a current example of fear from my own life.

In the last fifteen years, while my private practice has exponentially grown, the bottom fell out in 2016. As I mentioned in the Introduction, this was when the advent of Uber, Lyft, and other technology threw my practice into a downward spiral, with my gross income cut by about a third.

With an overhead that is relatively high, I found myself dealing with fearful feelings like never before. Negative thoughts would continually creep in. It was a rollercoaster of emotions. At times, the stress felt overwhelming.

But I combated those fears with a variety of techniques you're going to read about in the pages ahead--visualization, relaxation, and positive affirmations. I forced myself to visualize stomping out fear and replacing it with positivity. I prayed, I meditated, and I focused on positive future thoughts to overcome short-term negative moments in life.

Whenever I had a "low" moment driven by fear, I took an action in order to chip away at the goal, executing tasks that would ultimately lead me to big accomplishments in the future. Each action produced incremental progress. And each step forward generated more positive actions and enhanced the desire to achieve.

For example, I recently went to a networking event at a law firm and discussed the dilemma of my DUI practice dying because of Uber with the managing partner. I talked with him about my transitioning to a family law practice.

It turned out that he didn't have an attorney to refer family law cases, and he promised he would send cases to me. He intuited that I could transfer my established skills as a DUI/criminal attorney and utilize them as a family law attorney. That meeting gave me a positive boost, knowing that I now had a good referral base.

My vision today is to write this book, create an annual seminar, develop a family law practice, and maintain and improve my DUI/ criminal law practice.

That's a lot of change! And admittedly, a lot of fear.

But fortunately, I have an awesome office staff and support team. We have great chemistry and believe that our practice will rebound and flourish, just as much as ever. All we have to do is keep chipping away and taking action every single day to achieve the goals in our business plans.

* * * * *

It's easy to feel positive when life is going your way. But when things start to change and obstacles present themselves, that's when fear most notably presents itself. And that's when you really need to be tough.

The ultimate secret to dancing with fear is focused work—taking decisive action and accomplishing tasks toward your ultimate goal.

When you're actually engaged and "in it," rather than being nervous "about it," you are much less susceptible to the negatives of worry and anxiety. By focusing, you're calling fear's bluff. You're proving to yourself that you can step forward and do the next right thing.

You aim for the target. You stick to the plan. And by keeping your eye on the light at the end of the tunnel, you counteract feelings of discouragement, self-doubt, and the sense of being overwhelmed. You replace them with positive actions towards chosen goals.

Finally, remember, our profession is a people business focused on helping our clients attain the defense or advocacy they need.

You can and will make a difference.

Most of the time we get paid, while pro bono work allows us the chance to freely help others. In either case, people out there need your skills, insight, and time. They want their problems fixed--and you can do it. Knowing that helps erase fear, and giving to others, as you'll see in the pages ahead, is a great motivator.

REMEMBER THIS: *As you begin your solo practice, you may not succeed at first, but as Godin always says,*

"The willingness to fail on the way to reaching a bigger goal is the untold secret of success."

But there's one underlying secret to huge success that you can't do without it. It's . . .

3
Transform Your Thinking, Change Your Life

"When you expect the best, you release a magnetic force in your mind which by a law of attraction tends to bring the best to you."

– Norman Vincent Peale, *The Power of Positive Thinking* –

In business, some people think their greatest asset is their talent. Others credit their network of contacts, their educational background, their financial resources, or their staff. All those elements, of course, are important.

But your most important asset is nothing tangible. It's nothing you can hire, buy, or sell. It's your MINDSET.

This is your outlook on life, your basic way of thinking that permeates every one of your decisions and reactions. It's your established set of attitudes that powerfully affects your destiny. Your work, your health, and your happiness are all impacted by it. **That's why a positive mindset is the true secret to all achievement and success:**

- A positive mindset is encouraging and stabilizing
- It makes you feel enterprising and upbeat
- It motivates and gives you energy to accomplish your goals
- You feel inspired and energized rather than stressed and exhausted
- It gives you the strength not to give up
- It makes you look at failures as blessings in disguise

13

- You're solution-oriented rather than obsessed by conflicts
- It allows you to believe in yourself and your abilities
- It gives you genuine confidence

In short, **your way of thinking is like your calling card; the way you present yourself to the world.** It either draws people toward you or turns them away.

That makes your mindset the most consequential component of your life, directly affecting your success as a solo practitioner. In fact, I'd go so far as to say that **a positive mindset is an insurance policy for prosperity.**

Why?

Because your attitudes radiate outward to the world—to your staff, to your clients, and to other members of the law profession. You're more likely to WIN with this attitude. You'll win arguments, clients, and cases. You'll win friends and mentors.

"The right attitude will set the right atmosphere,
which enables positive responses from everyone in your orbit.
Our attitudes cannot stop our feelings, but they can
keep our feelings from stopping us."
– John C. Maxwell, *Developing the Leader Within* –

Everyone will notice this mindset because it shows on your face. You can't hide it. Your facial expressions are sure giveaways that reveal your attitudes and emotions. They're like radio waves transmitted through the air, picked up by everyone around you. And what you broadcast is instantly interpreted.

14

With a positive mindset, instead of transmitting a negative, cynical, unsatisfied, or lethargic signal, you're conveying a bright and buoyant one, energetic and enthused. That's a huge difference, and an indisputable component of success.

Above all, AVOID **resentful, angry, intolerant, and judgmental thoughts.** These emotions are your enemies. They sabotage your plans, filling you with ill intentions and self-doubt.

Of course, positive thinking doesn't mean you're impervious to life's realities—sad times, disappointments, and reversals of fortune happen to all of us. But it does mean that you approach these moments in a more constructive way.

That's because positive thinking builds the capacity to recover quickly from adversity and to adapt well to it. Rather than letting failure overwhelm you or drain your resolve, you rise from the ashes.

So whether it's family or relationship problems, serious illness, or workplace or financial stress, this approach allows you to "bounce back" to your most resourceful self.

Yes, you get knocked down by life, but you come back stronger than ever.

Armed with a positive attitude, you will:

- Cope better with stress
- Bring more optimism into your business, increasing revenues
- Enhance your creative thinking
- See the big picture and creative options
- Make better decisions under pressure
- Fuel positive expectation, making good things likely to happen
- Enjoy better marriages and friendships

And not least important: Positive thinking has been proven to benefit your physical health too.

- It lowers your blood pressure, heart rate, and cholesterol
- It combats depression
- It reduces the risk of death from cardiovascular disease and cancer
- It strengthens your immune system
- It wards off the common cold
- It prevents diabetes and hypertension
- It allows you to recover more quickly after surgery or illness
- It increases your pain tolerance
- It reduces stress-induced inflammation and levels of stress hormones such as adrenaline and cortisol

Wow! That's quite an incentive. Clearly, the attitudes of you and your employees will directly impact your firm's medical costs.

REMEMBER: *Health-related work losses are estimated to cost U.S. employers more than $260 billion each year.[6] So you're going to save time and money when you and your employees are physically healthier. And you can do it just by staying positive.*

But how?

---

6   https://www.ncbi.nlm.nih.gov/pmc/articles/PMC3128441/

4
8 Secrets to a Positive Mindset

SECRET #1 SELF-AWARENESS

Creating a positive mindset is like training for a marathon, a process that requires self-discipline, training, and tenacity.

Just as I did in Ironman, you build up your stamina and strength by pacing yourself through a structured regimen. And you do it daily.

You do the same thing with positive thinking by putting yourself in charge of what thoughts most dominate your mind.

While some people believe that their emotions, ideas, and attitudes are out of their control, it's simply not true. You can master your mindset by following the eight techniques described below.

And by doing this, **you're retraining your mind to perceive reality through the lens of positivity.** You choose your emotions and reactions. And the result, as you'll see, is a renewed sense of optimism, confidence, and energy that will directly impact the success of your business.

Let's start with self-awareness.

Every morning, when you look into a mirror, you see in the reflection everything about you. You take an inventory and notice if you need to comb your hair, wash your face, or shave.

4. 8 SECRETS TO A POSITIVE MINDSET

When you "look into the mirror" of your attitudes, take an inventory of what you're thinking and feeling and how that's affecting your quality of life.

Do you see a predominantly positive mindset driven by emotions like:

- love
- enthusiasm
- desire
- romance
- appreciation
- hope
- giving
- winning
- passion

That's a *thumbs-up* life!

Or do you see a negative mindset fueled by:

- hate
- apathy
- indifference
- dislike
- resentment
- despair

That's a raw deal.

The negative mindset is defined by toxic emotions that drag us down and stress us out.

It's horrible living on a diet of frustration, anger, and fear. It's the "junk food" of emotional nutrition, feelings that "tattoo" our minds and sabotage us. Under the spell of these emotions, we use words like "never," "shouldn't," and "can't," all game changers that diminish our potential for success.

That's why you have to work from the inside out to create genuine positivity; a winning attitude that will permeate everything you do. It almost guarantees stellar results. So it's worth paying a lot of attention to, even before you open the doors of your practice.

THE GOOD NEWS: *Positive and negative emotions can't occupy the mind simultaneously.*

Where there's faith, there isn't fear. Where there's enthusiasm, there isn't apathy. Put in another way, if you're dancing, you're not napping!

One or the other must dominate. And it's your choice. **That's why SELF-AWARENESS of your thought patterns is the first secret to cultivating positivity.**

You need to know your personality through and through. *What are your strengths? What are your weaknesses? What emotions fuel you?*

I can tell you that my strengths lie in my determination and work ethic, my ability to listen well to clients and understand their goals, my willingness to hire staff with different skill sets than my own, and in my litigation and trial skills.

But even more basically, I am highly self-motivated, often getting up at 4 a.m. to act on goals that I set for myself and my clients (because their goals are my goals). I'm both realistic and optimistic. And I always say that you have to know where you are in order to get to where you want to be.

So most mornings, what is your predominant mindset? Is it positive or negative? Do you begin the day with anticipation, or with a sense of dread? What kinds of thoughts are streaming through your mind?

The **Attitude Quiz**[7] is a great way to boost self-awareness to determine where you are in your positive/negative mind ratio.

Log on to **www.PracticeLawLikeAnIronman.comresources**
to take the Attitude Quiz for yourself

This will be the beginning to discovering your mission into who you are. Be honest with yourself and you'll get the best results. The best part about this quiz—there are no right or wrong answers.

Regardless of your score, there are times when we all succumb to thinking negative. In fact, **the #1 enemy of a positive mindset is negative self-talk.**

Self-talk means our inner voice, the conscious (and subconscious) things we think and say to ourselves that impact how we feel.

When I say negative self-talk, you know what I mean. It's that inner-critic chatter in your mind, the self-defeating voice that tells you all the things that are wrong in your world. *"I don't have enough. I don't do enough. I don't earn enough."*

You feel guilty about X and worried about Y. You compare and despair. You rewind the past and anguish about the future. You feel insecure and indecisive. You see pitfalls and potential problems in everything. Our heads fill up with a barrage of obsessive, debilitating thoughts that make us feel hurt, angry, frustrated, depressed, or anxious.

In short, it's a very bad mental habit that prevents us from fulfilling our potential. This inner critic must be silenced! But how?

---

7 https://www.ohsu.edu/xd/research/centers-institutes/oregon-institute-occupational-health-sciences/oregon-healthy-workforce-center/toolkit-kiosk/upload/Activity-11.pdf

SECRET #2 AFFIRMATIONS
Creating a New Mindset on Demand

A third-grade teacher in Philadelphia recently taught her class an inspiring technique for facing up to any life challenge. The class lesson was filmed and posted on Facebook.

She told her students to chant one simple phrase out loud, over and over again, with emphasis and emotion: **I'M GONNA PUSH THROUGH.**

This motivational mantra mastered by eight-year-olds went instantly viral, the teacher subsequently appearing on the Today show. And there it was, a powerful technique that a third-grader and all adults can master to counteract any obstacle or momentary setback.

THE LESSON: *When it comes to your state of mind, you can actually act yourself into feeling positive, even when you really don't. It's all within your power. It's like switching TV channels from one show to another. You can likewise change mental channels on demand, from negative to positive, whenever you want to.*

That third-grade teacher was providing a gift to her students... **the power of affirmations.** These are positive statements, words, or sounds repeated over and over again that declare your true intention to achieve whatever your outcome or goal may be.

Think of it as your mantra, your personal commitment phrase that sums up your internal drive for life. And when you say these words out loud, or write them down, you're reprogramming your brain to believe in them, which, in turn, can make them realities.

21

Not least important, if you're crowding out that toxic self-talk and replacing it with positive affirmations, you can overcome the chattering voice of negativity that fills your mind on a daily basis.

To begin the practice of affirmations, choose any words or sounds you like. There's no right or wrong. Brainstorm key words or phrases that ring true for you. The sentences are going to be short, believable, and focused.

Motivational speaker **TONY ROBBINS** calls these affirmations *incantations*; **"a pattern of words or phrases that you repeat with such intensity, consistency, and certainty that you feel them vibrating in your body and believe them."**

No matter what the task, your mantra is going to get you through it. You visualize those affirmations as not just coming true—but *being* true.

For example, a military mantra used by Navy SEALS during their training is "embrace the suck," as a reminder that the life of a soldier is often mindnumbingly repetitive and dull. It's focused on necessary tasks that may seem pointless, tiring, or lame. But you only have two choices. You can "embrace it," as SEALS say, "or roll over and die."

I can tell you that affirmations rewire our brains and have the power to change our lives.

"Your desire must not be a hope or a wish but rather a keen and pulsating <u>desire</u> which transcends everything else and is definite. Maintaining that state of mind known as a burning desire to win is essential to success."
– Napoleon Hill, *Think and Grow Rich* –

With the right affirmation:

✓ You can achieve greatness

✓ You can love and accept yourself for who you are

✓ You can have a healthy body and a tranquil soul

✓ You can believe in what you do

✓ You can have faith that everything is happening for your ultimate good

✓ You can be the architect of your life and have the ability to conquer any challenge

Here are a few examples of affirmations:

- Believe

- Dream bigger, reach higher, shine brighter

- I am magnificent

- I attract powerfully positive healthy people into my life

- I deserve to be happy

- I'm thankful for what I have

- I am the best

- I will do one new thing today

I'm ready to do whatever it takes

- I'm the creator of my life

- What's next?

- Let's do it

- All I need is within me

- I'm grateful every day

- Every day, every way, I feel better and better

- Things are going to work
- I will! I can!
- I feel energetic and healthy
- I will earn $20,000 this week
- I will earn $80,000 this month
- My client, _____, will be found not guilty
- I will have an excellent and persuasive closing argument
- I am prepared
- I will work hard and be smart
- I am an awesome person
- I am an awesome lawyer
- I will help my clients achieve their goals

Conversely, here are some commonplace deterrents leading to procrastination and delay:

- It's hopeless
- I'm helpless
- I'm overwhelmed
- I really should
- I wish I had
- I'll do it one day
- If only I had the time
- Maybe next year
- I'm not sure
- I'm not ready
- It won't work
- I can't do it
- It's too difficult

1

A defeatist attitude is your worst enemy, the epitome of negative thinking. This is a malignancy in thinking. As Seth Godin says,

"I define anxiety as experiencing failure in advance."

REMEMBER: *the words you use about yourself become realities. That's why incantations (and written affirmations) are so powerful in counteracting negativity.*

That's why anxiety must be combated continually by positively affirming that anything is possible.

When you find yourself upset or stressed, or reverting to feeling negative, you can also write out positive statements as bullet points for "right" thinking.

Be persistent. Do it every day. Say the words out loud with emotion. Repeat them morning and night until it's all been memorized. Use words that inspire or drive you forward in a positive direction. And know that you're in charge of what thoughts most dominate your mind.

SECRET #3 FAITH
Believe It and Make It Come True
"Faith is the head chemist of the mind."
– Napoleon Hill, *Think and Grow Rich* –

As we set out on a path of entrepreneurship, it's tempting to think we can control everything with enough hard work. We can't. Logistical preparation and discipline are essential, yes, but FAITH is your secret weapon. What your mind believes in and expects, it tends to receive.

We'll make this secret a quick one:

- Faith is a strong conviction in something that is not seen or tangible, but believing in it can make it real.
- Faith is your complete trust or confidence in a positive outcome.
- Faith is your ability to believe in something good.
- Faith leads to hope and overcomes fear.

You've got to have faith to make your solo practice thrive.

REMEMBER: The practice of law is a practice.
It's never perfect. You're always learning.
And you must be ready—and motivated for—change.
You have to have faith and keep the faith.

You have to believe in yourself, and remember that you became a lawyer for a reason. Dig down and focus on what that reason is. It might be the excitement of trying cases or solving problems for clients. Use that to bolster your faith, which will allow you to better accomplish your dream of being a successful lawyer.

So instead of filling your mind with thoughts of defeat or ineffectiveness, think thoughts to encourage and foster your success.

When you picture yourself as succeeding, that's faith. When you imagine your ability to conquer any challenge, that's faith.

Sure, you may have multiple law cases and a heavy workload, but with faith, you can and will get the job done. With faith you can delegate. With faith you can sub-contract. With faith you can find the focus and energy to economically accomplish your task.

Hold that vision firm. Never permit it to fade. Even when things may be going badly, keep that vision of success in your mind. And when a negative thought invades, swat it away with an incantation, deliberately voicing a positive affirmation to cancel it out.

Studies have proven that faith has tangible benefits that enhance your physical and emotional health:[8]

"All thoughts which have been emotionalized (given feeling) and mixed with FAITH, begin to immediately translate themselves into their physical equivalent or counterpart."
— Napoleon Hill, *Think and Grow Rich* –

Faith encourages healthy lifestyle choices and behaviors

- Faith reduces stress
- Faith reduces coronary artery disease
- Faith reduces blood pressure
- Faith improves emotional health
- Faith leads to more social connectedness

ALONG THE WAY: Minimize obstacles or difficulties in your imagination. See them as solvable, not inflated by fears. Take one step at a time, and you won't feel overwhelmed.

AND REMEMBER: *One component of faith is persistence... the daily discipline of forging ahead, even when you don't feel like it.*

---

8 https://www.psychologytoday.com/blog/more-mortal/201406/5-scientifically-supported-benefits-prayer

Setting up a solo practice, as the next section will show, is a multi-faceted, complex task. To do it, you need to maintain a daily structured regimen.

Every time you check off another task on your to-do list, you've demonstrated an act of faith.

And every time you ask someone for help or support, you've demonstrated an act of faith. In fact, when you find others to believe in your goal (accessing their faith), it strengthens your own resolve, giving you new energy to persevere.

AS NAPOLEON HILL WROTE,

"Faith is the starting point of all accumulation of riches." When you master it, you master fear. And you become invincible.

AS HILL SUGGESTS: <u>Write out a statement of your vision.</u> This is your major purpose, the goal that you have real faith in. Drill down on it. Focus. The subconscious mind will translate it into reality. We'll talk about a vision statement more in the next section of the book.

A leap of faith, of course, takes courage. It takes the willingness to face risk and uncertainty, a subject we covered earlier. A solo practitioner must be an Ironman or Ironwoman.

All in all, the faith muscle can be strengthened by persistent, continuous action toward achieving your objective. Faith can also be strengthened by the act of **<u>making a list</u>** of everything you've already overcome and accomplished in your life. Seeing this list in black and white is empowering.

So for 30 minutes a day, focus on believing that you will create a successful small firm and a lucrative practice that fits you. Create a clear mental picture of you being that person, and persistently hold it in your mind.

You need to have faith that you have the ability to achieve your purpose, and faith that your dominating thoughts will result in a tangible result.

That's faith in action.

SECRET #4 RELAXATION

A Merry Heart Doeth Good

It's amazing how our bodies reflect what we're feeling emotionally. If we're stressed-out, angry, or afraid, our shoulders, back, and neck immediately become tense and tight. And that's why emotional stress is one of the leading culprits of physical distress, especially lower back or neck pain and chronic headaches.

Did you know that 100 million Americans suffer from chronic pain daily, and this exacerbates irritability and negative thinking? It makes us feel anxious, short-tempered, and overwhelmed. And it zaps our energy and diminishes our efficiency.

That's why another secret to creating a positive mindset is the ability to **RELAX**—to be free from tension and anxiety. We need to strive for peace of mind. We need time to decompress, loosen up, and unwind.

The health benefits are amazing. Relaxation studies have proven that:

- Relaxation protects your heart
- Relaxation lowers the risk of catching a cold
- Relaxation boosts your memory

- Relaxation lowers the risk of stroke
- Relaxation reduces depression
- Relaxation helps you make better decisions
- Relaxation keeps your weight under control

Take a break from negativity. It's like going on a diet. Avoid gossiping or talking negatively about family members, friends, or business associates. Stop watching so much negative news on TV and social media. Focus on something that will lift you up rather than depress you. Watch something that will make you thankful, not resentful. It's your choice, and you can do it.

From a physical standpoint, just the simple act of **DEEP BREATHING** is an effective way to quiet your mind and calm your emotions. Even **RELEASING THE TENSION IN YOUR JAW** fosters relaxation.

And there are hundreds of other things you can do to relax:

- Take a nap
- Listen to your favorite music
- Stretch
- Hydrate
- Take a drive
- Ride a bike
- Take a spin class
- Get a massage
- Bask in the sun
- Go to church
- Take your kids bowling
- Plan a party

- Play with your dog
- Talk to a counselor
- Play golf
- Play a video game
- Read a book
- Listen to a motivational tape
- Pray
- Meditate

It's up to you. Any of these activities can get you into a more relaxed, hopeful, optimistic state of mind. You'll find yourself saying and doing the right things more and more. It's a habit, and you can get into it.

But no matter what, find a way to relax and unwind, have some **fun and share some *laughter*.** In fact, scientists have proved that **LAUGHTER dramatically boosts your mood as it can erase fear, anger, anxiety, and depression.**

Health-wise, laughter:[9]

- Lowers blood pressure
- Reduces stress hormone levels
- Works your abs
- Improves cardiac health
- Boosts T-cells
- Triggers the release of endorphins
- Produces a general sense of well-being

What could be better than a free activity that conditions the heart muscle, exercises the lungs, boosts the immune system, and even increases adrenaline and blood flow to the brain?!

---

9 http://www.mayoclinic.org/healthy-lifestyle/stress-management/in-depth/stress-relief/art-20044456

So find something to laugh about and stop wasting energy on anger, fear, frustration, and worry. When those emotions surge up, ask yourself:

"Is this really worth the cost of what it's doing to me emotionally?"

It never is.

In those moments, we must will ourselves to quietness. There are dozens of ways to do it. Some people like meditation or yoga, a long walk or a brisk run, or listening to music or a relaxation tape; others prefer massage or a steam bath. Some relax by watching TV, or by gardening or golf.

So whether it's ping-pong or watching the Travel Channel, prayer, meditation or acupuncture, or playing video games, find a way to **LET GO.**

As NORMAN VINCENT PEALE suggests:

Visualize all those negative emotions being dropped overboard of a ship, dissolving away, disappearing in the horizon. Worries, fears, and insecurities are only thoughts—and you can let go of them. Relax them away.

Then, once your mind is empty, focus on your favorite things—the smell of your favorite meal cooking, (or for me, the amazing scent of flowers and nature when I'm out on the lava rock or the beaches of Hawaii), the laughter of your toddler, the touch of your spouse, the sounds of the ocean, the light of the moon. These images are the keys to peace and serenity.

Especially at bedtime, empty your mind and release all the tension in your body. Be thankful for being set free from the bondage of negative thinking and stress. Tell yourself: "I'm filling my mind with thoughts of good will, forgiveness, and faith." Allow yourself to feel hope. Express love to those around you. Have courage. And believe in positive expectancy.

SECRET #5 CHOOSING THE RIGHT PEER GROUP

Who You Spend Time With Is Who You Become

We've seen the power of self-awareness, affirmations, faith, and relaxation. But you can't stay positive all by yourself, no matter how reflective and proactive you might be.

That's why another secret to a positive mindset is **surrounding yourself with the right network of people who can inspire and support you.** This is your PEER GROUP—the friends, family, and colleagues who are most influential in your life.

Finding reputable mentors and peers is essential for brainstorming ideas and fueling motivation. It sets you up for success as you actively seek out others who already have it. This expands your perspective and ups your game.

Having the right peer group:

- Raises your standards
- Holds you accountable to your goals
- Provides instant resources to colleagues and clients
- Offers social interaction
- Gives safety and support in times of crisis

Once engaged with those you most respect, you bounce ideas around and ask other lawyers what they think. How they would approach the issue? Inevitably, you gain valuable information.

I can tell you that throughout my career I've sought out and looked up to numerous attorneys who were highly skilled in DUI and criminal defense. And I felt gratified when attorneys looked up to me as I earned a track record as a reputable lawyer and an expert witness for field-and-breath-testing issues.

Be grateful to the lawyers in your chosen peer group, and be sure to thank them for their time and energy in helping you. And whenever you can, refer business to them.

In my own practice, as I said earlier, I'm currently carving out a new niche in family law. So I've reached out to several established family law attorneys in Cincinnati who have helped me in building my practice. They identified the key players in this field and educated me about what I need to know about the family court system, the personalities of the judges involved, etc.

One family lawyer and his paralegal even presented an in-house seminar on family law to orient my staff to this specialty. I not only wrote a thank-you note, but also gave them a generous gift certificate to one of their favorite restaurants, which I know they appreciated.

Such collegial relationships become powerful and invaluable, so you need to nurture those relationships and give back to them. Host events or parties, and invite business colleagues, neighbors, family, and friends. Include in your peer group people with a wide range of contacts who operate successfully in their fields. I'm talking about people who are not lawyers, but great business people, whether in the banking, accounting, real estate, or insurance fields, among others.

These are the people who have influence over your standards and expectations. These are the people who can inspire and challenge you, who can support you by demonstrating their ability to stay positive and productive. They can also hold you accountable for your goals and give you insight into how they achieved their success. **These are the winners.**

So deliberately seek out their company. By networking with them, your skill sets and business prospects will improve. So will your mood and self-esteem.

Conversely, if you surround yourself with a peer group of negative thinkers who have low aspirational goals, this will only reinforce your own negative thinking.

It's true that misery may love company, but that is not the kind of company you want to keep. **You're a victor, not a victim.** People who are downbeat and discouraged are not going to motivate you.

So don't hang out with pessimistic, negative thinkers. These are the doubters, cynics, and haters who do nothing but complain and see what's wrong in life. They're like vampires who suck the life out of you. They're the enemies of success.

If friends, family, or colleagues become doubters, learn to politely dismiss their advice and judgments. Their negativity may be a projection of their own fears. Maybe they don't have the guts to do what you're doing. Don't hold it against them. But know yourself. Follow your intuitions. Remember, you're working out of the box, not in the comfort zone. So it's inevitable that some people around you may question your ability to succeed.

Ask yourself:

- ✓ Who's going to inspire, challenge, and push me to the next level of success?
- ✓ Who would be the ideal person to spend more time with? Who do I want as my peer?
- ✓ Who will I give that power to?

Choose your peer group wisely, because who you spend time with is who you become. Who you connect with shapes your destiny.

SECRET #6 THE ART OF GIVING

The Holy Grail of Sales and Marketing

Often, as we begin a solo practice, we're focused on what we need and what we need to get—resources, referrals, financing, and staff support. And it's easy to forget that **one of the prime secrets of a positive mindset is the ART OF GIVING.**

When you contribute anything -- your time, energy, attention, or a gift -- it's a gift enjoyed twice; once by the recipient and once by you. True giving means you do it with no expectation of a return. Yet ironically, one of life's most basic laws is that every single act of generosity will multiply and return to you many times over. The more you give, the more you will receive in human kindness.

What can we give?

- Donate your talents
- Give someone a lift

- Offer money
- Provide a recommendation or referral
- Make someone laugh
- Contribute to a charity
- Give a surprise
- Send an invitation
- Give affection
- Give compliments
- Offer good advice
- Give encouragement
- Give forgiveness
- Donate blood

There are so many ways to give. The list is endless. And any act of kindness fuels positivity and empowerment. You just feel good when you do it.

One of my favorite books is The Go-Giver: A Little Story About a Powerful Business Idea by Bob Burg and John David Mann. The protagonist of the story is an ambitious young salesman named Joe who yearns for success.

Joe meets a series of "go-givers" that includes a restaurateur, a CEO, a financial adviser, and a real estate broker. They all teach him that your true worth is determined by how much more you give in value than you take in payment, that your income is determined by how well you serve others, and that the most valuable gift you can offer is yourself.

All in all, Joe learns that he must change his focus from getting to giving—putting others' interests first and continually adding value to their lives. Doing this ultimately leads to unexpected returns.

It's all based upon the wise proverb: **"Give and you shall receive."**

In a solo law practice, giving is particularly important when it comes to referrals—it's the holy grail of sales and marketing.

When you or someone else refers a potential client, this gives you a tremendous advantage over the competition—because you have effectively been "pre-qualified" in the eyes of the prospect. By providing a referral, you are transmitting that you care enough to try to help. That action also demonstrates to your employees that giving is a part of your firm's mission.

There are a few simple rules of the road for "giving" when it comes to referrals:

- Assess the client's best interests, considering their personality, budget, and extent of legal service.
- Give one sure-fit recommendation (and a few others if necessary).
- Give your time to make an introduction via phone, email, or meeting.
- Refer to your other clients whenever possible, being perceived as a moneymaker for others.

Be someone who gives thought, time, care, and attention in all your affairs, both business and non-business. When you offer a positive vibe to others, it will rebound to you in their excellent performance.

In that way, helping others helps you. This will result in more referrals and new business coming your way.

In our profession, of course, one potential vehicle for giving is pro bono work. It makes a lawyer feel satisfied to represent those who would otherwise not be able to get the help they need. You're freely giving your expertise for a greater purpose than income.

SECRET #7 BEING THANKFUL

Count Your Blessings, Not Your Sorrows

The next secret to cultivating a positive mindset is: **BE THANKFUL.** A grateful mind is a positive one, which is why putting gratitude in your attitude produces tangible physical and emotional benefits.

Gratitude is the prayer of the enlightened. It is an essential component of a positive mindset. It gives you an instant feeling of well-being. It makes you feel happier and more satisfied in all areas of your life, and reminds you of the fantastic people in your life and of the things that you already have.

Gratitude

- Opens the door to more relationships (showing appreciation wins you new friends).

- Improves physical health (fewer aches and pains, extends longevity).

- Boosts psychological health (reduces toxic emotions like envy and resentment, frustration and regret).

- Enhances empathy and reduces aggression

- Benefits sleep

- Increases self-esteem (and reduces comparing and despairing oneself to others).

Research shows[10] that **recognizing what you're grateful for trains your brain over time to become happier—and happier people are 31 percent more productive.** In a business environment, they produce better sales figures, they're more resilient, and they have less burnout.

---

10 http://www.health.harvard.edu/healthbeat/giving-thanks-can-make-you-happier

In fact, heartfelt emotions like appreciation produce what one study called "harmonious heart rhythms" that are considered to be indicators of cardiovascular efficiency and nervous system balance.

Conversely, experiencing anger, frustration, anxiety, and insecurity causes heart rhythms to become incoherent or jagged, causing our hearts to function less efficiently.

Express your appreciation for the things you're thankful for, such as your physical health, your family and friends, and all the things in life that you value most.

Write down 25 things you're grateful for. First and foremost, your family and friends, their physical health, your home, your job, a great workout, a walk in nature, the taste of your favorite meal, your favorite wine or craft beer, the view from your porch, your dog or cat, or the pleasure of air-conditioning on a hot day. Include everything and *anything* at all that means something to you. And remember to express thankfulness for the modern conveniences we take for granted; the luxuries that millions before us never imagined.

- What would we do without modern dentistry? (wooden teeth?).
- How did Abraham Lincoln cope without a cell phone or an internet connection? He just did.
- How do people in underdeveloped nations live without indoor plumbing or the flick of a switch to light up the bathroom? They just do.
- The next time you accidentally cut your finger, appreciate the other nine of them. (It seems we only remember to appreciate the basics until something goes wrong).
- When you pick up the phone, remember that prior to 1876, nobody had one.
- When you drink a glass of spring water, remember that 783 million people in today's world don't have clean drinking water.

How lucky are we?

In your solo practice, when you earn a new client, be grateful, and thank them directly. I created a personalized thank-you card that has my firm's name on it. I send it to a client right after they hire me, thanking them for their business and their trust in me.

You can also write notes to the dozens of people in your world that you are grateful for (or to), whether it's a friend, colleague, family member, teacher, neighbor, physician, or a waiter at your local coffee shop. Everyone loves to get a personal note (better than an email).

Make sure that you give back to your referral sources as well, whether it is a mentor or colleague. I always invite my colleagues and social friends to my law office bar. *Yes, I have an actually bar that I had made and crafted for the fun of it.*

It all started in 2010, when I purchased an 1830's building with an attached carriage house, which I turned into an Old English pub. I named it *Filibusters*. I host happy hours, fundraising events, and parties there, using it as way of creating goodwill and thanking defense attorneys, prosecutors, colleagues, staff, and friends (though since a great deal of my practice is DUI defense, I generally don't invite those particular clients to the bar.)

Goodwill=Gratitude

It's a way of showing how thankful I am to people who have helped and supported me along the way. It's also fun. I've hosted Super Bowl and tailgate parties at Filibusters; all a way of giving back to those who have given to me.

I also treat my mentors to lunch or dinner, and they often do the same. It's a give-and-take relationship. And it's the same thing when it comes to staff. Tell them how much you appreciate what they do. Treat them to lunch. Remember their birthdays. Send a get-well card. If they do a great job, give them a generous bonus.

1

In short, appreciate everyone in your world, and be thankful. When you do, they will appreciate you. And do it because you want to, not because you have to. When your giving is genuine and heartfelt, it remarkably comes back to reward you in one way or another.

And outside the work environment, allow gratitude its moment by intentionally acknowledging the so-called little things that aren't so little at all. It could be something as seemingly trivial as someone holding a door open for you, or an eager dog climbing into your lap, the taste of a perfect ripe tomato, or swimming in the ocean. You name it. It can be anything at all, nothing earth-shattering, but a perfect moment to be grateful for.

SECRET #8   VISUALIZATION
A Dry Run for Life

Many entrepreneurs believe that their success will be a result of one great idea, the right connections, a combination of luck and talent, or the perfect financing. But while these factors are all crucial, they're not enough.

That's why the final and perhaps most important secret to creating a successful solo practice is **VISUALIZATION:** *a mental technique that uses your imagination to create a picture of your future as you wish it to be.* By visualizing a detailed picture of the final result, you plant the seeds for achieving it.

Visualization is a mental rehearsal. It's like a dry run for life. It allows you to practice...to feel your way through scenarios before you actually take steps to make them real. You create goal pictures in your mind; images of having or doing whatever it is you want.

You'll read more about it in the next section of the book. For now,

REMEMBER: *Imagination is to visualization what oxygen is to breathing. One can't exist without the other. So our ultimate success as solo practitioners depends upon the ability to form a clear mental image of something that doesn't yet exist.*

It's like kids playing "pretend." They build imaginary worlds that seem completely real to them. We, as adults, can do the same thing, creating mental scenes of exactly the kind of life we most want.

I compare it to dreaming. When you're sound asleep, the things that happen in your dreams seem absolutely real. You're transported to another time and place. You can see, feel, taste, touch, and smell the action. Conscious imagination can work the same way. As **NAPOLEON HILL put it, it's as if your imagination is the**

"receiving set through which ideas, plans, and thoughts flash into the mind."

These flashes are known as hunches or inspirations. It's like a sixth sense that's actually more important than any one skill. **The power of visualization has many benefits:**

- Helps you focus better on what you really want.[11]

- Inspires and motivates you to get the job done.

- Boosts your mood by using positive, pleasant imagery to alter negative emotions.

- Increases alpha brainwaves

- "Tricks" your subconscious mind (which can't tell the difference between a memory and a vivid visualization).

---

11 http://www.essentiallifeskills.net/visualization.html

- Builds self-confidence (as you rehearse success in your mind).
- nhances relaxation.
- Boosts possibility and desire (while cancelling out fear and conformism).
- Increase focus and desire.
- Rehearses problem-solving (with new ideas and hunches).

A positive visualization is like a "telegram" to your brain. What you're doing, as stated above, is tricking your subconscious mind by seeing yourself already in possession of the desired goal. That positive intention will activate the creative side of your mind, making whatever it is you want more likely to happen.

"You must focus and concentrate until your desire becomes a burning obsession. You have to see and feel yourself already in possession of whatever it is you want. 'Plain' unemotional pictures won't influence the subconscious mind, so you must mix emotion and faith into the picture you create."

– Napoleon Hill, *Think and Grow Rich* –

But the key catalyst to it all is emotion and a burning desire. **As NAPOLEON HILL wrote:**

"Your subconscious mind recognizes and acts only upon thoughts which have been well-mixed with emotion or feeling."

That you can't learn. It has to be built in to your motivational psyche. So if you have a throbbing ambition for a successful outcome, that desire plants the seed for your career to grow.

If you're a person of faith, call it an "idea session" with God. Meditate or pray on your next move, on how you can create the greater good with your gifts and abilities. The more you visualize your idea, the greater chance that it will become real.

For example, as a DUI attorney, I wanted to challenge a law in Ohio that prevented defense lawyers from disputing and questioning breath test evidence. Even if it took going to the Ohio Supreme Court, I vowed that I would have that law overturned.

To affirm my determination, I wrote down on a 3x5 card that I would be the attorney who argued to overturn that Ohio Supreme Court ruling (in State v. Vega). I taped that card up on my dresser drawer where I could see it every day. I finally got the right case and took it from the trial court all the way up to the Ohio Supreme Court in order to eliminate this ridiculous law. It took years. But in the end, the Supreme Court ruled in my client's favor 7-0. And while the law was not overturned, it was worded so that attorneys could challenge breath test evidence at trial.

Writing down this goal, putting the written mantra on my dresser, and seeing it every single day helped me achieve this ambition of significant new case law.

Visualization and writing out your target aspirations is essential, not just for your practice but for your other personal goals in life. You've got to picture yourself succeeding in your mind before you actually succeed. You're harnessing 100 billion brain cells and getting them to work in one purposeful direction.

AS RALPH WALDO EMERSON SAID:

"A man is what he thinks about all day long."

So what most fills your thoughts? Hopefully not plots of revenge or payback, but rather ways in which you can be productive and spread some happiness to others.

Beware... when you find a skeptical, undermining, or negative thought invading your "air space," consciously eject it—as *The Power of Positive Thinking* suggests -- and substitute it with a happy and positive thought. Replace those negatives with your true desire.

Some people may find this practice a little odd—but it's like exercising a muscle. The more you use it, the stronger it gets.

In short, when you expect positive results, you get them. And what you focus on, you attract, no matter what your background or profession.

As we saw earlier with affirmations, the subconscious mind will accept the thoughts that you repeat with emotion, and will transform your mindset accordingly.

Visualization is the key to achieving whatever it is you want, whether it's a thriving law practice, a healthier body, or increased confidence.

Fueled by the power of visualization, let's now map out the nuts and bolts of setting up a solo law practice that's perfect for you.

For additional resources that will facilitate the planning of your practice as well as your implementation process, visit the Ironman Resource page for more info, www.PracticeLawLikeAnIronman.com/resources

PART TWO

20/20:
The Magic
of Visualization

5
The Picture of Your Practice as it's Meant to Be

"If you don't know where you're going, you'll probably end up somewhere else."

-Yogi Berra-

As we saw in the previous pages, there are eight secrets to positivity, all of which are tools to powerfully create an Ironman mindset. Next, you're going to use that mindset to solidify the ideal practice for you.

Some of you will have already chosen your law specialty or specialties by the time you read this. But even so, over time, as your interests expand and market conditions change, your areas of expertise may change along with it. You're never locked into just one thing.

No matter what, for true fulfillment, you must find meaning in the specialty or specialties you choose, rather than being solely propelled by financial considerations.

As an experiment, identify one legal case that leads you back to the reason you became a lawyer in the first place:

- What about it was so compelling?
- What about it made you care?
- How did you feel after the case was closed?
- What knowledge came out of the case?

- What complementary strategies did you develop?
- What new people did you meet?

Perhaps it was a case that saved a family from foreclosure, or one that helped an immigrant remain in the U.S. Maybe a drug addict received the treatment he or she needed, or an alleged drunk driver or criminal suspect received a proper defense and was found not guilty.

Whether it was a movie deal, a corporate merger, or something much smaller, this was a case that was meaningful to you.

* * * * *

For me, there was a case in 2003 that indelibly reminds me why I became a lawyer. I was the defense attorney for a 36-year-old man charged with three counts of assault against three undercover police officers. My client vehemently insisted that he was innocent; a victim of excessive force. The police investigation was sloppy and their statements inconsistent, but with no plea bargain offered, we proceeded with a oneweek jury trial.

My client had a previous criminal record. But through my efforts, he was found *not guilty* on all charges. It was the case that fueled my ambition as a defense lawyer.

Another case that strongly resonated with me was my defense of a woman charged with possession of heroin. The police case was founded on the assertion that my client gave consent to search her car. This was untrue.

At the trial, I entered into evidence a videotape showing my client insistently telling the police that she would not consent to the search. Yet that Cincinnati police officer blatantly lied about the sequence of events.

While my client was technically guilty, the judge reluctantly granted my motion to suppress and later dismissed the case due to the violation of the Fourth Amendment, which protects citizens against unreasonable searches and seizures.

2

John Adams once said of our criminal justice system,

> *"A society gains more by protecting innocence than by punishing guilt."*

In short, **no defendant should be convicted by corrupt law enforcement.** This case stood out to me, and reinforced my determination to give each of my clients a vigorous and passionate defense.

It was these kinds of cases that fueled my ambition as a defense attorney.

So for you, <u>zero</u> in on the emotion attached to the case that drew you to it like a magnet. Pairing up genuine interest with an emotional payoff is the key to creating the right practice for you.

In the end, the secret to creating a thriving practice is to:

- ✓ Fuel it with passion
- ✓ Build it with solid business practices
- ✓ Sustain it with powerful people skills

So which area(s) of specialty seems like the one(s) best suited to your legal temperament?

- Bankruptcy law
- Business (corporate) law
- Civil rights law
- Criminal law
- Entertainment law

50

- Environmental law
- Family law
- Health law
- Immigration law
- Intellectual property law
- International law
- Labor (employment) law
- Military law
- Personal injury law
- Real estate law
- Tax law

Take two minutes and fill out this (admittedly not highly scientific) *DiscoverLaw.org* quiz[12], which gives a snapshot of what specialty best matches your personality and temperament:

http://www.discoverlaw.org/considering/quiz/

Optimally, your choice should be determined by **who you are and what you want.**

It will be based upon your:

- Passion
- Personality
- Income requirements
- Family history
- Genuine interests
- Contacts
- Marketability potentials
- Geographic location

---

12 http://www.discoverlaw.org/considering/quiz/

And in this decision, don't forget "fatherly advice." *Literally.* My dad, who was a civil litigator in a rural county in Illinois, knew how much I wanted to do trial work in a more urban environment. So in the early 1980s he advised me to move to a bigger city and to choose a specialty that would build my name and allow me a greater income.

Fortunately, I got into the Hamilton County Prosecutor's Office, which covers Cincinnati and its suburbs. The eight years spent there prepared me for eventually switching hats and turning to a more lucrative pursuit as a criminal defense attorney.

For any lawyer, having long experience on both the plaintiff and defendant sides is a key asset. For me, they are really just flip sides of the same coin. Randy Freking—a mentor of mine at one of the major firms in Cincinnati—specialized for years in defending corporations against employee lawsuits. He eventually switched hats too, and today he is one of the leading plaintiff employment attorneys in the country.

So when you're assessing which area of law to pursue, your decision will be based on many of the factors listed on the previous page. Not least important, confer with law professors, practicing lawyers, friends who know you best, and family members too, just as I did (whether they are lawyers or not).

FYI, someone I know who was addicted to TV crime shows as a kid went into criminal law, which was a natural for him.

In the end, it's a very personal decision and a major one. In making it, you have to think long-term and outside the box, using the most dynamic tool of all.

6
How Visualization Really Works

As we saw in the last chapter, visualization can be powerfully used to create detailed pictures of what you want your life to be. Using this technique, you create mental images of the future in order to make them a reality. Your goals become completely attainable.

As Steven Covey says in *The 7 Habits of Highly Effective People:*
All things are created twice – first in the mind, and then in reality.

I sat down and read Covey's book cover-to-cover in 1990, just after taking the bar exam. As he suggested, I started writing out goals in several circles of my life, and wound up with two legal pads full of notes!

Years later, I pulled out those pads again and realized that I had accomplished almost every single objective I'd written down. I passed the bar. I got into the prosecutor's office. I ran for public office (I lost, but it was still a great experience). As I mentioned earlier, I qualified four times for the Ironman Triathlon World Championships in Hawaii. I got married to a beautiful woman (inside and out) who is an awesome wife. I have two amazing sons. I have great friends. I have a solid relationship with my God. I'm still working on becoming a millionaire (I'm close, but not quite there).

What you visualize is what you become.

The goal is to have an idea, think and act on it, and write down the tasks in order to get to your objective. Visualize being successful, and have faith that you can do it. You do this for your practice... and for your life. Even when circumstances change in life, you can visualize a new solution. For example, all that training and pounding (because of running) caused me to have a hip replacement at age 47. I couldn't run anymore! At the time, this was devastating. It was very tough, particularly because my wife and I enjoyed running together. But coping with change in a positive way was necessary.

Today, I can still work out and I'm healthy, but no more triathlons. The upside is that I get to spend more time with my family. So I readjusted my mindset to a different channel in order to change my habits and have a happy life. Changes in life happen, and you must go on in a positive direction.

> **REMEMBER...***you're in charge of what thoughts dominate your mind. You can either voluntarily feed your subconscious with positive impulses, or permit the negative to dominate.*

How do you do it?

It's simple...you put yourself into a relaxed position. You can lie down on a couch, stretch out on your favorite chair, or climb into a hammock, whatever you like. Close your eyes and relax your body. Feel each of your muscle groups letting go, unwinding all the tension and stress.

Now crowd your mind with positive images for the solo practice you want to create.

- What would your ideal law practice look like?
- How would it thrive?
- How would you feel?
- What would your greatest contribution be?
- What amount of money would you earn?
- What service would you provide to be worthy of it?

In my case, as a trial attorney, I always visualize my voir dire before the trial even starts. I imagine the opening statements, the crossexaminations, the interchanges with the judge, and closing arguments. Then I visualize the jury verdict in my client's favor, and by doing this, I've had a great number of successes.

You can also use the visualization technique to:

✓ Picture the kinds of clients perfect for your practice.

✓ Imagine them paying your fee.

✓ Imagine the perfect law office facility.

✓ Project your earning potential:

☑ Lock down a financial figure in your head.

☑ Write it down and keep it close (in your wallet).

☑ In a relaxed state, positively affirm it repeatedly: "I will make X amount this week, Y amount this month, Z amount this year. I will earn my potential. I will earn the money I deserve."

I can tell you that I've earned the fees I've visualized, and won the cases in court that I imagined I would. So using visualization benefits your clients, creates great work product, and helps you deal with judges and adversaries.

I also visualize creating team chemistry in my firm, positively affirming that I will find and hire the right employees. I visualize powerful marketing plans too, including the successful use of social media, websites, advertising, and media appearances on radio and TV.

I also use visualization to see myself as someone who wants to get better and be better. For example, I've spent thousands of dollars on continuing legal education seminars to enhance my craft and improve my work product for me and my staff.

It all starts with having a compelling vision that you believe in; one that you can imagine.

"There is a deep tendency to become what your mind pictures, provided you hold the mental picture strongly enough."

– Norman Vincent Peale, *The Power of Positive Thinking: 10 Traits for Maximum Results* –

You can do the same thing on the personal front:

- What would an ideal evening with your partner look and feel like?
- How would you act?
- What would you say?
- How romantic and sensual would the connection be?
- How would you feel the next day?
- What would having this connection mean to your future?

Now, when it comes to imagining your solo law practice, here are some warm-up questions:

- ✓ What would your solo practice consist of?
- ✓ What would you have to do to create it?
- ✓ How would it thrive?
- ✓ How would you feel when it did?
- ✓ What amount of money would you earn?
- ✓ What service would you provide to be worthy of it?
- ✓ What would your greatest contribution be?

By visualizing and thinking about a meaningful future, you make it real. And that repeated vision of your ideal practice actually programs the subconscious part of your brain to bring it to fruition.

What you tell your mind, it believes. And what it believes becomes a reality.[13]

---

13 http://tinybuddha.com/blog/your-reality-is-a-reflection-of-what-you-believe-you-deserve/

Professional athletes and performers are masters of visualization. As many have said: *What happens out there is a result of what happens in here.*

In fact, studies show[14] that visualization increases athletic performance by enhancing **motivation**, **coordination**, and **concentration**.[15] It also aids in **relaxation** and **helps reduce fear and anxiety.**

That's a very potent pill, which is why star athletes like **JERRY WEST, MICHAEL JORDAN, LARRY BIRD, TIGER WOODS,** and **ROY HALLADAY** have all used visualization to improve their performance. You can use it too. I did.

During my competitive swimming and triathlon days, I used visualization to the max. My coaches taught me to relax my body and visualize my performance down to the last detail. I visualized qualifying for and competing successfully in the Ironman Triathlon World Championships in Hawaii.

Even in law school, I swam 27 miles over a 12-hour period for charity, and I visualized enduring and succeeding throughout that entire swim, constantly affirming positive mantras in my mind, as well as focusing on relaxation and technique.

After that marathon (plus) swim, I felt the satisfaction of accomplishment and the satisfaction of raising money for the American Diabetes Association and the Phi Alpha Delta Legal Fraternity.

Although I was not a world champion at the Ironman World Championships, my performance still benefited greatly by visualizing an image of a successful race and time.

But no matter what your goal, athletic or legal, the practice of visualization is the same. Visualize the details and visualize enduring and succeeding.

---

14 https://www.psychologytoday.com/blog/flourish/200912/seeing-is-believing-the-power-visualization
15 https://digital.library.txstate.edu/bitstream/handle/10877/5548/EKEOCHA-THESIS-2015.pdf?sequence=1

- **MUHAMMAD ALI** gained a psychological advantage over opponents by always seeing himself victorious long before the actual fight, thereby becoming a champion with "an inner picture" of success.

- **JIM CARREY,** as a struggling young actor, used to envision himself being the greatest actor in the world, sought after by film directors. He made out a check to himself for $10 million when he was flat broke, a fee he would later earn for *Dumb And Dumber.*

- **TONY ROBBINS** was broke, overweight, and near bankruptcy before he envisioned himself as a life coach with the ability to motivate others, healing people at hotel and radio venues and ultimately building a $30 million per year empire.

- **MICHAEL JORDAN** was a meticulous planner, visualizing every shot before a game began. He confided that his greatest strength wasn't his height or physical skill, but his power to focus and imagine making the perfect shots.

- **MICHAEL PHELPS,** an Olympian with 23 gold medals, has been visualizing since he was seven years old. He "watches" what he calls his "videotape" of the perfect swim each night before going to sleep to mentally map out his strategy for the next day.

- **OPRAH WINFREY** pulled herself up from poverty and childhood sexual abuse (repeating to herself, "my life won't be like this"), using vision boards with cutouts of pictures, drawings, and phrases of things she wanted in her life. She climbed the ladder and became a media mogul, a healer, and communicator to millions.

- **ARNOLD SCHWARZENEGGER** visualized winning the Mr. Universe title for many years, and later used the same process to create a vision of who he wanted to be. He then lived that picture as if it was true, becoming a movie star, real estate tycoon, and governor of California.

- **BEYONCÉ,** the daughter of a hairdresser and a Xerox sales manager, became a Grammy award-winning recording artist, actress, and songwriter by keeping her life's objective always front and center, placing a picture of her Academy Award next to her treadmill so she can see it daily.

- **LINDSEY VONN,** one of the most successful female ski racers in American history, always visualizes the run before she begins, drilling it 100 times over and over in her head, picturing exactly how she'll take the turns.

2

They did it and so can you!

VISUALIZE YOUR SUCCESS. Assume it. Make it your obsession. Paint in all its details. Get your senses involved. Write it down. Picture it in your head. Say it out loud. Stamp it indelibly in your mind.

Here's How to DO IT:

✓ Go somewhere quiet and private, with no distractions.

✓ Stretch out on a couch, chair, bed, hammock, on grass or on a beach, wherever you're comfortable.

✓ Take several deep breaths, and relax your muscles completely, unwinding tension and stress.

✓ Now close your eyes and visualize your solo practice (forget practicalities for now).

✓ Visualize your law practice with as much detail as you can (below are some opening questions).

✓ Now add all five senses to the picture and FEEL it.

✓ Practice twice a day for about ten minutes each time.

As you practice, the picture you create will become more and more detailed. Ask yourself:

2

- What area of the law is most compelling to me?
- Which aptitude of mine most powerfully matches it?
- Which specialty will be most fulfilling emotionally?
- Is my vision realistic?
- Does my vision of the practice have a back-up strategy built into it for setbacks?
- What will be my firm's raison d'être—its reason for being?
- What will my firm do to help people?
- Can I take a model from another firm and enhance it?
- What market will I serve?
- What kind of clients do I want walking through the door?
- Why should they choose my firm, above all others?
- How can I provide superior quality and service?
- What marketing message would attract these clients?
- Where will my office be located?
- What does it look like?
- How many employees will I have?
- What kinds of people will I hire?
- What values are most important to me?
- Am I a catalyst or a drill sergeant?
- Do I command my staff or convince them?
- Will I take in a partner, or go entirely solo?
- How many hours a week will I work?
- How will I balance my work and my personal life?
- What is the office's annual gross revenue?
- What is my compensation?
- What will I do with the money?

- How much *pro bono* work will I take on?
- How will I be a force for good in the community?
- In the next five years, how will the practice grow?

Using all these questions as a springboard, as time progresses, you can flesh out in great detail the practice of your dreams. Hold that vision until it is absorbed by your subconscious mind, as it will be. Let all the details of your vision repeat themselves, day and night.

Then relax the mind and "clear it" until the full picture "flashes" into your consciousness. As we said earlier, these flashes are hunches, what I sometimes call *inspired intuitions*. They are internal animations of what we most desire, like the motion pictures of our fantasies. If you can dream it, you can make it come true.

As you conjure up what you most desire, if you find negative, skeptical thoughts invading the air space of your mind, you can annihilate them by repeating your affirmations—OUT LOUD.

By doing this, you shut off the flow of negative thoughts, crowding them out with the positive ones. Eventually, those resourceful positive emotions will dominate your mind so that negatives can't even enter it.

REMEMBER: *As you fill out the picture of your unique vision, don't be imprisoned by conventional thinking...what others think you SHOULD be doing, or what others ARE doing.*

You're creating your own practice. Metaphorically speaking:

- You're *Amazon*, not a bookstore
- You're *Uber*, not a taxi
- You're *iTunes*, not a record store

You are an independent entrepreneur. A visionary leader-in-training. As such, you need to fuel your imagination by exposing yourself to as many ideas as possible.

To create a forward-thinking roundtable of ideas, I suggest you do the following:

✓ Study the most successful law practices in town.

✓ Invite a lawyer to lunch.

✓ Network with people outside the law but within your target industry.

✓ Join community groups like the Rotary Club to talk to leaders.

✓ Attend events listed on sites like LinkedIn, Facebook, and Meetup.com.

✓ Read trade magazines and attend conferences to harvest ideas.

✓ Access your peer group, and mine them for contacts and ideas.

✓ Confer with mentors.

✓ Check your files or notes for forgotten "too soon" ideas that fit now.

7

Creating Your Vision and Mission Statements

A ship can't leave the port without all of its provisions and a clear-cut itinerary route. Neither can you. As a solo practitioner, you need to know exactly where you're going and how to get there.

HOW? By creating **vision** and **mission** statements that motivate and inspire you, and that allow you to take control of your practice. By putting both statements in writing, you're memorializing them for your staff while clarifying your own thinking.

What is a Vision Statement?

A <u>VISION STATEMENT</u> describes a picture of your firm as it *will* be, in its future, successful state. It's an overall blueprint of what you're building; of what the completed "house" will look like. The best vision statements are succinct summaries of the idealized objectives of your firm. They offer a long-term perspective that inspires and motivates employees.

It should include both **tangibles** (types of practice areas, number of clients and employees, gross profits, and number of offices) and **intangibles** (the feel and atmosphere of the firm).

To summarize: A <u>vision statement</u>

✓ Defines the optimal desired future state of your firm—your mental picture of what you want to achieve over time.

✓ Provides an inspiring roadmap as to what your firm is focused on achieving in five, ten, or more years.

✓ Functions as the "North Star"—the ultimate goal that motivates your employees over the long term.

✓ Should be written succinctly in an emotional manner that makes it easy for all employees to repeat it at any given time.

Here are some questions to get you started:

- What do you want to ultimately achieve with your practice?
- How do you want the world to see your practice?
- What do you want to be known for?
- Where will you locate the practice?
- Who are your ideal clients?
- Why will they hire you rather than the competition?
- What's the one word that clients will associate with your firm?
- What do you want your clients' experience to be like?
- What kind of culture will your firm have?
- What kind of colleagues do you want?
- What are your financial goals for your practice?
- What kind of lifestyle will your firm support?
- What will your firm allow you to do with the rest of your life?

- What will inspire you?
- What will be your guiding beliefs and values?

REMEMBER: *An effective vision statement should look forward to least three to five years, or even ten. It should also identify the major issues and long-term goals needed to achieve the vision, including strategies in support of those goals. It should address the questions addressed in these samples:*

2

Here's the vision statement for my practice in Cincinnati:

OUR VISION is to create a thriving, referral-based law practice in southwest Ohio and northern Kentucky, a firm that will gross over $1 million per year, emphasizing the areas of DUI, criminal defense, and family law. We will establish a compelling online social media presence, branding us as the most experienced and knowledgeable firm in our concentrated areas of practice. We will provide responsive hands-on customer service, with meticulous attention to detail, and fees that will be competitive but reasonable, reflecting our position as the go-to firm for superlative results.

Here's another example of a vision statement from a small firm, Leo Law Firm, LLC, in Huntsville, Alabama:

OUR VISION is to provide our clients with skilled legal advice in a timely and efficient manner. We strive to handle each matter with accountability and responsiveness, as if we were representing ourselves. We focus our attention on the legal aspects of our client's business so that our clients can focus their attention on the success of their business. Our vision reflects our values: integrity, service, excellence, and teamwork.

OPTIONAL: In your own firm, you can schedule vision statement meetings periodically so everyone can participate in refining the firm's message.

You can organize and divide the topics as follows:

- Governance
- Administration
- Economics
- Practice management
- Growth
- Firm culture
- Marketing
- Technology
- Facilities and equipment
- Geographic and substantive service areas

How to write a MISSION STATEMENT?

A <u>MISSION STATEMENT</u> describes the firm's purpose in the present; it's very reason for existence. It answers the question, *Why should I hire you to represent me?* It's a simple three or four sentence summary that defines the **purpose**, **values**, and **priorities** of your firm.

It includes the work you're doing now, the clients you do it for, and the qualities that differentiate your firm from its competitors. It should be not only lofty and idealistic, but catchy too, as it serves as a mantra for the firm.

To summarize, a <u>MISSION STATEMENT</u>:

- ✓ defines the purpose of an organization.
- ✓ answers three questions about why an organization exists:

☑ __WHAT__ does it do?

☑ __WHO__ does it do it for?

☑ __HOW__ does it do it?

It's written in the form of a sentence or two, but for a shorter timeframe (one to three years) than a vision statement. Also, it's something that all employees should be able to articulate upon request.

Here are some questions for developing your mission statement:

- What do we do? (what is your firm all about?)
- Why do we do it? (why are you practicing law?)
- What distinguishes us from other law firms in terms of size, style, and approach?
- Who are the clients?
- What geographical markets do we serve?
- How will the firm's culture be reflected in service to clients?

We have created an online version of the above questions so you can easily begin to create your own mission statement interactively by simply answering these questions.

To access the online form, visit
www.PracticeLawLikeAnIronman.com/resources

Using these two documents will help ensure you are on your way to creating one of the most valuable assets of your business.

8
Your Firm's Core Values

The foundation of both your vision and mission statements is what I call your firm's **CORE VALUES—the traits and standards that will form all your behaviors and actions.**

Core values govern relationships, guide business processes, reflect the practice's identity, and become a factor in all your decisions.

In short, it's your firm's moral and ethical code that determines the right path toward fulfilling your business goals.

- **Which attributes do you most value?**
- **Which personal qualities do you want to be known for in the legal community?**

For example, the international law firm Faegre Baker Daniels lists as its core values:

- Honesty and integrity
- Excellence
- Hard work
- Teamwork and collaboration
- Mutual respect and firm-mindedness
- Diversity and inclusion
- Service to our communities

These core values are your *standards,* and they generally fall into three categories:

✓ CONTRIBUTION – your firm's mentoring and training, business development, and involvement in the community.

✓ BEHAVIORAL – your firm's commitment to teamwork, to excellence, to being available and accessible to clients, to treating others with respect.

✓ CHARACTER – honoring commitments, being true to your word, enhancing the firm's reputation, exhibiting the highest ethical standards.

The concept behind establishing formal written **values** is that they will serve as a philosophical and work culture foundation so that all decisions can be tested and measured against the stated principles. You and your staff commit to applying these ideals in your daily practices and in relationships with clients and with one other.

Other typical law-practice core values include:

■ OWNERSHIP – a responsibility for profit and the efficacy of the firm.

■ LEGACY – a commitment to leave the firm better than you found it.

■ RESPECT – for people and their dignity.

■ SERVICE – to clients and to one other.

■ EXCELLENCE – aiming for the highest-quality legal representation and professionalism.

■ INTEGRITY AND HONESTY – reliability, trustworthiness, transparency.

■ TEAMWORK – a collaborative cooperative approach among lawyers and staff.

- **CONTRIBUTION** – a commitment to earn one's spot on the payroll each year.
- **ACCOUNTABILITY** – agreeing to be bound by the reasonable standards and expectations expressed in the core values.

2

* * * * *

The benefits of articulating core values are many. Solo firms that occupy a suite of law offices with other practices will establish relationships based upon trust and respect, which will allow them to:

✓ Cross-sell

✓ Refer business back and forth

✓ Share resources

✓ Make sure work is being done by the right lawyers

In short, the implementation of core values will grow the firm, expand client relationships, and improve profitability. Sure, the positive changes might not be immediately apparent, but firms that live their values will ultimately treat clients better, develop lasting relationships, and keep them coming back.

9
Ready for an Action Plan

Once you've established your vision and mission statements and your core values, you're ready to create an ACTION PLAN; **a detailed strategy outlining activities needed to reach your goals.** This is the nuts-and-bolts of setting up a law practice, which you will read about in the upcoming chapters. They outline the sequence of steps that must be taken, and activities performed for your game plan to succeed.

As Arthur Greene and Sandra Boyer explain in *The Survival Guide to Implementing Effective Law Firm Management Strategies,* **your written strategic plan should include the following:**

- Core values, mission statement, and vision statements.
- A summary of the opportunities and obstacles ahead and how they may impact the practice.
- A prioritized list of goals:
  - Focus on only a few goals so you're not overwhelmed.
  - The objective should be short and measurable.
  - The objective should tell you what is going to be done and how the goal will be achieved.
  - It should include a timeline for implementation, with specific tasks assigned to hard deadlines.
  - Hold yourself and others accountable to deadlines.

2

As you develop your action plan, rely upon your MASTERMIND ALLIANCE; **a group of 6-10 people who comprise your peer group.** You're going to glean from them years of invaluable experience. As we discussed earlier, these are the supportive and accomplished friends, colleagues, and mentors whom you most respect. They already possess significant experience in handling the systems referenced above. Their knowledge is invaluable in expediting your set-up. Arrange to consistently meet with them, at least twice a week (more if possible), until you have jointly perfected the necessary plans to establish your practice.

The motive of masterminding is to access the knowledge of each member for the benefit of the whole group. As Napoleon Hill noted in *Think and Grow Rich*, a "mastermind alliance" is designed to encourage you to follow through on your plan and purpose. It was practiced by such figures as ANDREW CARNEGIE, HENRY FORD, and THOMAS EDISON. *And it will work for you.*

By brainstorming:

- ✓ You receive quality feedback
- ✓ You access proven strategies
- ✓ You gain clarity of direction
- ✓ You become accountable for actions to be taken
- ✓ You celebrate large and small successes along the way

REMEMBER: *Your imagined vision of your business will now become a concrete reality.*

And it should include these goals:

- **FINANCIAL:** What is your ultimate money objective, and how will you get there?
- **EMOTIONAL:** What impact will your practice have on your well-being and on everyone who comes into contact with you?

- **CLIENTS:**
  - Who are your target clients?
  - Why should they hire you?
  - What benefits will your practice offer them that no one else will?
  - How can your network of family, friends, colleagues, bankers, and commercial real estate and insurance agents help you to procure new clients?

- **EMPLOYEES:**
  - How do you find candidates who want to grow with your firm?
  - How do you develop employee talent?
  - How do you teach them people skills and customer service?

- **BUSINESS:**
  - What image do you want to project in the minds and hearts of employees, clients, and your community?
  - What systems will you develop to hold the team accountable?
  - Who will implement, design, and create the systems?
  - Who will manage them?

Before turning the page, visit the Ironman resource page where you can access an online version of the questions above as well as additional resources that will facilitate the planning of your practice.

Visit www.PracticeLawLikeAnIronman.com/resources

THE NUTS AND BOLTS OF SETTING UP YOUR PRACTICE

10
Creating a Hyper-Smart Office With a System that Tracks Everything

"Three rules of work: out of clutter find simplicity; from discord find harmony; in the middle of difficulty lies opportunity."
-Albert Einstein-

Now that you have your vision and mission statements solidified and your core values established, you're ready to create an **ACTION PLAN—a detailed guide that outlines initiatives needed to reach your goals.** We're talking about a sequence of steps that must be taken, and activities performed, for your game plan to succeed.

Beyond legal theory, you're going to think strategically about every aspect of creating a solo practice, using legal, management, and client-relations skills to do it.

As we saw, you're not just a lawyer anymore. You're an entrepreneur. **AS SUCH, YOUR MISSION IS TO ACCESS:**

- Personality strengths
- Ambition
- Decisiveness
- Faith

- Persistence
- Organized planning

While the best thing about being a solo practitioner is the sense of freedom and empowerment that comes with it, the down side is that you do not have a corporate umbrella to protect and manage your interests.

There is no personnel department, no fleet of receptionists, paralegals, or secretaries, and no extended support staff or colleagues.

3

INSTEAD: *You must become a law practice manager and the firm's prime administrator.*

You will, of course, delegate tasks as your firm expands, assembling a team that may later include an associate lawyer, a legal secretary, a paralegal, a receptionist, and/or an office manager. At first, you'll be wearing multiple hats, not just as a lawyer, but as the firm's chief executive, financial, and information officers rolled into one. In these roles, your responsibilities include overseeing all corporate governance. **Your goal is to have established SYSTEMS and PROCEDURES for all office operations and client relations.**

When I need to **create a system,** I sit down with my staff, and we brainstorm, creating a checklist from beginning to end on how to do something to expedite the practice. The end goal is to establish a protocol that anyone in the office can follow and implement with reliable results. So if an employee leaves, another can come right in and be trained using your procedures or "systems" manual.

For example, I created a motion-to-suppress system that my staff now uses to help me prepare for pretrial motions to suppress evidence hearings. It is exceptionally detailed.

I have also created a system for what I call my "reasonable doubt charts." This is a bullet point outline of every reason a jury should doubt a particular piece of evidence that comes in at trial.

My staff uses notes from the file and pretrial motion transcripts to create the charts for purposes of preparing for trial. I can look at the charts, add to them or delete from them as I see fit, and then be ready to go to trial and argue that the state has not met their burden of proof, which is proof beyond a reasonable doubt.

All in all, systems like these are incredible timesavers. My paralegals know how I prepare for trial, and can do it themselves in order to get me prepared. Meanwhile, I can spend time doing other things for clients, such as marketing the firm and making the firm prosper.

As described in *The E-myth Attorney: Why Most Legal Practices Don't Work and What to Do About It,* the result is a dependable turnkey operation that works "predictably and automatically" every time. This means that with the right training, anyone brought into your practice can successfully reproduce the same results.

In other words, think of your practice as a piece of software, fully integrated, automatic, and logical. Administrative headaches of the practice are minimized. Established systems will reduce anxiety, increase consistency, and allow you to focus your mental energy on practicing law and other revenue-generating tasks.

You are essentially managing systems, not people.

Creating such systems take **time**, **energy**, **money**, and **advance** planning. It's a process, not an event. But, one step at a time, as described in the pages ahead, you're going to **create operating procedures for:**

✓ Delivery of legal services

✓ Client and case management

✓ Document control

✓ Timekeeping and billing

✓ Accounting

✓ Filing systems

✓ Preparation for litigation

✓ Technology updates

✓ Marketing and client development

✓ Communication skills:

- Active listening
- Client service
- Personnel interviewing
- Presentation skills
- Networking
- Relational skills
- Case management
- Delegation
- Ethics

To break it down further, for every task in the firm, there should be a system for the following:

✓ Office operating procedures manual

- For this, there is no need to re-invent the wheel. Ask a colleague to give you a copy of their office manual, and then revise it as desired. It should include:

- ☐ Standard procedures/policies for practice
  - ◆ Tardiness
  - ◆ Absences
  - ◆ Sicknesses
  - ◆ Holidays
  - ◆ Overtime
  - ◆ Mileage
- ☐ Dress
- ☐ Demeanor and attitude
- ☐ Collaboration tools, allowing staff to work on documents and assigned tasks and to track milestones remotely, such as:
  - ◆ www.imeetcentral.com
  - ◆ www.onedrive.live.com
  - ◆ Google Docs
  - ◆ Drop Box
- ☐ Medical benefits
- ☐ Hiring and firing
- ☐ Interview protocol and standards
- ☐ Performance reviews

✓ **Docketing, calendaring, tickler system**

✓ **File organization**

- • Alpha/numeric
- • Centralized/decentralized
- • Opening file procedures
- • Closing files
  - ☐ Procedures
  - ☐ Retention

☐ Storage

    ☐ Destruction

✓ **Document maintenance**

- Offsite–safety deposit box
- Computer backup
- Fireproof files

✓ **Forms used in practice**

- Client interview form
- Engagement/non-engagement letters
- Written fee agreements
- General client correspondence, notices
- Client survey form after conclusion of representation

✓ **Client billing procedures**

- Regular monthly statements even if no amount due
- Detailed billing statement
- Expense billing
- Costs to be billed
- Legal assistant/paralegal time
- Time telephone expenses
- Duplicating expenses
- Computerized legal research
- Mailing costs
- Collection policy
- Credit cards for payment

✓ **Accounting Procedures**

- Bank account reconciliation
- Cash Flow Statement/Accounts Receivables/Payables
  - ☐ Aging Review

- Expense Approval System, i.e., counter-signature requirement on checks

✓ **Client Relations Policy**
  - Client intake and conflict checking
  - Setting appointments, introducing staff
  - Telephone and email protocol
  - Corresponding with current clients
  - Developing leads and referrals
  - Telephone communication with clients
  - In-person client protocol and greeting
  - Staying in touch with former clients
  - Survey at conclusion of representation
  - Keeping clients informed
  - Sending copies of documents
  - Communicating about fees
  - Maintaining office equipment/technology

✓ **Legal Correspondence**
  - Sorting/distributing/filing
  - Depositions
  - Obtaining medical records and other evidence
  - Filing documents and day-to-day file handling

✓ **Marketing and Business Development**
✓ **Contact Database, differentiating:**
  - Friends
  - Relatives
  - Colleagues
  - High school contacts
  - College classmates
  - Law school classmates
  - Court personnel
  - Former clients

3

- Current clients
- Prospective clients
- Service and operational personnel
  - ☐ Staff
  - ☐ Accumulated business cards
  - ☐ Conference attendees
  - ☐ Lawyers in your community
  - ☐ Business vendors
  - ☐ People you meet in various organizations and clubs

✓ **Contact Database, including:**
  - Email
  - Fax
  - Street addresses
  - Telephone numbers
  - Website addresses
  - Social media handles
  - Personal information regarding
    - ☐ Family
    - ☐ Interests
    - ☐ Birthday
    - ☐ Previous legal concerns
    - ☐ Client needs and goals

Well, that's certainly a mouthful of systems! As we cover each of them, **consider the following:**

- **What is the optimal end-goal for each system?**
- **Is this activity really necessary?**
- **Do we need additional training to accomplish it?**
- **How can we use our existing office technology?**

- How does this procedure provide value to clients?
- How can this task be performed most efficiently?
- Who or how many staff members should be assigned to perform it?
- What are the steps to performing each function?
- How can we out-perform our competitors, differentiate ourselves, and attract new clients?
- Can we simplify this task or set of tasks?

3

Identity Standards

Underlying all office systems are what I like to call your IDENTITY STANDARDS, **which reflect the ethics of the firm and your professionalism and seriousness.** Your firm's identity is reflected in a myriad of ways:

- GRAPHIC STANDARDS—the style and quality of your logo, business card, stationery, and advertising graphics in both print and social media.

- OFFICE STANDARDS—the sights, sounds, and smells of your office should reflect a pleasant professional working environment via furnishings, cleanliness, organized desks, and office equipment, appropriate lighting, etc.

- TELEPHONIC STANDARDS:

  - A professional, pleasant live greeting sets the right tone and sends a marketing message.

  - Receptionist should follow an agreed-upon script for answering calls.

  - Create a protocol for taking messages or putting calls directly through.

- Record a congenial professional voicemail (or answering service greeting) providing options for emergencies:
  - ☐ Don't say you're on the phone
  - ☐ Don't say you're away from your desk

- **EMAIL STANDARDS:**
  - Choose a template complete with contact information and a marketing-based signature.
  - It should coordinate with your printed stationery and reflect the mission and quality of your firm.
  - The email system should have an automatic spell-check and a protocol for reviewing all emails carefully before pressing the "send" button.

- **DRESS CODE STANDARDS**—The attire chosen by you and your staff sends an instant message about the professionalism of your office, so it must enhance your overall brand. Remember to dress a little better than your market.
  - What image are you projecting?
  - How does that image impact your clients' impression?
  - What does it say about your ability to deliver?

If and when you need additional help and support for any of these issues, reach out for expert advice.

To access downloadable resources that will help you along your journey, visit the Ironman resource page, www.PracticeLawLikeAnIronman.com/resources

11
Location, Location, Location!

Now that we've identified the entire landscape of systems required for a viable practice, let's focus on the first primary decision to be made... **where to establish your law office.**

As a rule of thumb, a typical space for a solo law practice is 400-750 square feet minimum. This includes space for your office, a secretarial area, reception, storage, and room for basic office equipment, such as a copy machine. To save on costs, you can consider renting an inside office space with no windows.

And remember: If you're not renting in a suite with other lawyers, as we will discuss, you'll need a larger space for a conference room too.

Offices can be configured in a variety of ways. Unless you have a natural aptitude for it, you'll want to figure into your budget the cost of an **office designer or consultant to map out:**

- Placement of furniture
- Open work areas
- Cubicles
- Private areas for support staff
- Conference room and reception space
- Area for collecting books and journals

Create a move-in office budget covering the costs of:

- Computer equipment and wireless service
- Technological consultation
- Rent and/or mortgage payments
- Utilities
- Outlets and wiring
- Staffing (in-house and outsourced)
- Security systems
- Renovation of space
- Office supplies
- Telephones
- Credit card machines

To pinpoint an appropriate rented or purchased office location, it's essential to:

✓ Go where your targeted clients are (research demographics and economic data by ZIP code):
- What will attract a client to this locale?
- Where does that ideal client go to socialize and network?

✓ Define the ratio of lawyer to geographic population:
- Who are my major competitors in this area?
- How can I pinpoint them?
- How do I distinguish my practice from theirs?

✓ Consider proximity to:
- Municipal, state, and federal courts
- Public transportation for staff and clients

- Restaurants for client entertaining
- Law library

✓ **Find a disability-accessible facility.**

✓ **Factor in your lifestyle (e.g., the distance between your office and the location of your home and your social and recreational habits).**

✓ **Lease or buy an office that has space for a proper reception and conference rooms and restrooms.**

3

✓ **Choose a building or freestanding structure that is visible and that matches the defined image of your firm.**

✓ **Choose an office with convenient parking spaces for you, your staff, and clients at a fixed price.**

✓ **Contact a competent realtor to make sure you are getting a fair market rate for your space; and request a competitive market rent analysis from the realtor.**

✓ **Before signing your lease, do a background check to confirm that your landlord is credit-worthy. You do not want to invest in space when the landlord might be struggling to keep the lights on or pay his mortgage.**

✓ **Sign an OFFICE LEASE or RENTAL AGREEMENT that includes:**

- Access to the office at night and on weekends.
- Per square-foot cost based on furnished or unfurnished.

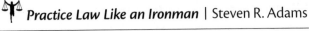
- The option of having the landlord build out your space and pay for it.
- Right of first refusal on additional space.
- Thermostat controls for air conditioning and heating.
- Sufficient electrical outlets and option to install more.
- Carpet cleaning and or replacement.
- Painting and cleaning.
- Cleaning the curtains or blinds, or getting new ones.
- Minimal maintenance, e.g., trash removal, janitorial service, carpet maintenance, etc.
- Verify what expenses are in your lease or not included in your lease, i.e., included in the rent payment:
  - ☐ CAM (common area maintenance)
  - ☐ Taxes or insurance
  - ☐ Utility payments
    - ◆ If the above expenses are included, you want to cap those expenses while negotiating the lease to avoid paying more per square foot later on if the property changes owners.
- Time the start date to coordinate with furniture delivery, announcements, and setting up your address in different publications.
- A clause that allows you to add space and services as needed, should you blend your practice into a law suite practice.
- Room for storage; particularly closed paper files.
- Nearby parking for you, your employees, or clients.
- Have an overall growth plan built into the lease. You do

not want to be tied to the space if you are going to outgrow it.

- Negotiate flexibility on your lease. Set your lease for a period of time, but always be able to get out of the lease.

- You may have to sign a one-year lease, but have a provision to go month-to-month after the first year.

- Cap the amount of real estate tax at the time you sign your lease. If a new owner comes along and real estate taxes increase, you don't want to be charged for the additional taxes that the new owner incurs.

✓ **Consider aligning yourself with a law suite; an already-established group of practitioners who act as sounding boards and provide potential referrals while sharing expenses.**
You share:

- Administrative employees:
  - ☐ You don't pay payroll, accounting, taxes, or workers compensation.
  - ☐ Availability of non-lawyer personnel to assist with word processing, filing, or special projects.

- Reception space

- Conference rooms (find out how their use is prioritized)

- Kitchen

- Internet

- Photocopy equipment

- Mail handling

- Automated voicemail system

- Break room supplies

- Cleaning crew service

- Web conferencing
- Legal library

Advantages of joining a law suite:

- Reduced monthly expenses
- Flexibility to terminate occupancy
- Flexibility to expand or contract space, facilities, and services
- Predictable fixed monthly expenses
- Minimal maintenance.
- Access to secretarial pool
- Access to other lawyers for advice and referrals

Disadvantages of joining a law suite:

- Potential incompatibility of practice mix
- Receptionist indifference
- Potential lack of air-conditioning/heating on weekends or holidays
- Potential gaps in the law library covering your area of practice
- Limited or no storage facilities for closed files
- Omission of your name from the building directory or suite entrance, though this can be negotiable

Now that you have a blueprint of what factors to consider in choosing a location, your efforts to find the right office begin. This is like shopping for a home or apartment. You want multiple choices. So, as luck would have it, we have created a downloadable pdf for you

Visit the Ironman Resource Page for your copy today.
www.PracticeLawLikeAnIronman.com/resources

12
Equipping Your Office from A to Z

As summarized in an *Entrepreneur* article titled *Office Essentials Checklist*, whether you're equipping your first office, sprucing up a new location, or re-stocking your current one, this checklist will help you determine and track which furniture, equipment, technologies, and supplies you need to help your practice run perfectly.

- Desks and office furniture (consider buying good-condition used, rather than new).

- Ergonomic chairs (with wheels and tilt and height adjustments for staff), and two to four straight-backed chairs for clients—professional and comfortable chairs.

- Wastebaskets throughout the office.

- Floor pads for desk chairs.

- Lamps (if necessary).

- Conference table.

- Chairs for conference table.

- Bookshelves.

- File cabinets for both current and archive files.

- Coat rack and umbrella stand.

- Postage scale (I recommend Pitney Bowes: 1-800-522-0020).
  - Establish UPS and FedEx accounts:
    - ☐ Always ask the client their preference for sending or receiving information.

- ☐ Postage and express delivery service expenses can be reduced with appropriate use of email and fax.
- Postage meters can be rented on a monthly basis. Check out these models:
  - ☐ Mailstation2 ($25 monthly)
  - ☐ PostBase Mini ($18.95)
  - ☐ IN-360 ($45.00)
  - ☐ WJ20 (Usually below $25.00)
- For personal cards or thank you notes, use a regular stamp on the envelopes.

- **Small table in reception area for magazines, including *ABA Law Practice,* books you have written and your field of practice journals or periodicals.**
- **Artwork for walls.**
- **Books and periodicals:**
  - Use electronic law libraries like Westlaw (1-800-762-5272) or Lexis Nexus (1-888-AT-LEXIS).
  - Use your local law school.
  - Use your courthouse law library.
  - Buy *The Lawyer's Guide to Fact-Finding* on the Internet, second edition, by Carole A. Levitt and Mark E. Rosch.
  - Buy used books from law schools.
  - Use the library in your office suite if there is one.
  - Use your state bar association's electronic library.

Next, the choice of computer software is hugely important in setting up your law practice. Choose from one of these, among those listed on Capterra.com: [16]

---

16 http://www.capterra.com/sem-compare/legal-case-management-software?headline=Top%20
10%20Law%20Practice%20Software&gclid=CKXQ8J-3rtMCFdCCswodpIIFZA

The Top Ten Law-Practice Database Software Options

1. Clio
2. PracticePanther
3. AbacusLaw Cases
4. MyCase
5. Legal Files
6. Firm Central
7. Smokeball
8. CosmoLex
9. Marketing 360
10. Rocket Matter

Visit the Ironman Resource Page for your top-ten list today, **www.PracticeLawLikeAnIronman.com/resources**

While you can study in-depth summaries, each and every one of them will allow you to **efficiently operate:**

- Case and client history
- Case management
- Contact management
- Document management
- Word processing
- Email
- Spreadsheets
- Time and billing/accounting
- Presentation (such as PowerPoint)

- Calendaring and docketing
- Conflicts checking
- Document assembly
- **Virus protection**
- **Voice recognition**[17]
- **CYBER SECURITY**
  - Anti-virus
  - Anti-spam
  - Anti-spy
  - Anti-theft
- **Security checklist protocol**
  - Windows and Office updates enabled and current.
  - Antivirus enabled, scheduled scans and updates.
  - Firewall enabled.
  - Strong password, 12 characters consisting of upper, lower, numbers and symbols.
  - Passwords changed regularly.
  - Weekly education business-grade network firewall (nothing purchased at Staples, Best Buy).
  - Confidentiality agreements with vendors.
  - Technology acceptable use policy for staff.
  - Data backup for more than just files and folders.
  - Data-restore testing.

Other important things to consider...

✓ **Buy a prepackaged personnel secretarial testing kit, which includes:**
  - Dictation information

✓

---

17 For voice recognition, the current iPhone 7 has an app allowing you to install Dragon on your iPhone or use an app called Voice Memos in which you talk directly into your phone and have it later transcribed by staff

✓ **Interview and evaluation forms for testing secretaries**

- Retain an office-supply vendor, considering:
  - ☐ Cheapest source
  - ☐ Fastest source
  - ☐ Minimum order
  - ☐ Shipping protocol (preferably free)
  - ☐ Discounts available
  - ☐ Set up a charge account

✓ **Create your office supply order list**

- Visit www.PracticeLawLikeAnIronman.com/resources for a complete list.

✓ **Preorder checks and deposit slips for your:**

- Trust account (IOLTA)
- Business checking

✓ **Order a credit card machine** (work with your bank to set up a credit console).

✓ **Use LawPay**—the best in payment processing, tailored to law firms, creating online billing and client portals for easier client transaction and bookkeeping.

✓ **System for library/legal research:**

- Online legal research provider
- Purchase new or used law books
- Local law library
- Law school library
- Courts library
- Internet research:

✓ System for shredding legal files:

- Purchase a paper shredder (or set up an account with a confidential paper shredding company).

- Consult state laws and guidelines before destroying client files.

- Create a document destruction policy:
  - ☐ Procedure for closing files
  - ☐ Procedure for storage of closed files
  - ☐ Schedule for periodic review of closed files
  - ☐ Designation of individuals responsible for reviewing files
  - ☐ Legal records retention schedule detailing periods for documents to be destroyed and guidelines for files that should never be destroyed.
  - ☐ Procedure for informing clients of file destruction policy upon engagement.
  - ☐ Procedure for contacting clients regarding closed files before destruction.

13
TIP: Reduce Clutter and Practice E-mail Management

Once your practice is all set up, you're going to quickly see how rapidly clutter can fill your office, with the build-up of meeting notes, letters, files, invoices, court documents, CLE notices, law practice journals and even takeout menus (!) on your desk.

As much as possible, utilize electronic filing, because too much clutter has a negative impact on your ability to focus and process information.

A study conducted by neuroscientists at Princeton University examined people's task performance in an organized versus disorganized environment. The results demonstrated that **physical clutter in your surroundings competes for your attention, resulting in decreased performance and increased stress.** It also slows you down, and it can be mentally exhausting.

- Put the paper files away until the appointment date and time arrives.

- Move closed files to an out-of-the-way or off-site storage area, or better yet, scan, save on the Cloud, and dispose of the physical file.

- Check state conduct rules for file storage time length and/or destruction.

- Return original documents to clients, disclose in advance that you intend to dispose of their paper files if permitted.

- The only things on our desk are files used daily, or files for today.

- Office supplies should be in shelves or drawers within reach.

- Utilize vertical space (hang shelves/wall pockets/bulletin boards).

- **Opening mail, separate into the following piles:**
  - Do (items that require action).
  - Decide (decisions that need to be made that are not client-related).
  - Pay (bills to be paid).
  - Read-and-toss mail.
  - File (items that need to be saved in the client's file or for your records, but do not require other action).
- **Don't become dependent on paper reminders.**
- **Organize your files into electronic files, such as action folders, master project lists, etc. Some suggestions:**
  - Evernote, a cross-platform, online archiving and note-taking software.
  - Diigo, a Cloud-based knowledge management program that allows you to take personal notes and highlight text information on web pages.
  - InstaPaper
  - Delicious
  - Reeder
  - Pocket
- **Switch from paper fax to eFAX to eliminate:**
  - Monthly telephone company bills
  - Long-distance charges for faxes
  - The cost of a fax machine, paper, toner, maintenance and repairs. Instead, use:
    - ☐ RingCentral (ringcentral.com)
    - ☐ eFax (efax.com)
- **Use an electronic calendar with reminder alerts.**

- Buy a business card scanner, insert into contact database or CRM, and discard paper cards.

- Skim through journals and periodicals for articles of interest, to be scanned by your secretary.

- For articles found online, use Evernote, Microsoft One Note, or similar apps to clip an article for future reference.

Email, mentioned on the checklist above, is obviously an invention that has revolutionized communication, but it can be a burden as well. Each day, hundreds of new emails—many of them junk mail—flow into our systems. I know lawyers who have literally thousands of emails in their inboxes with no dedicated system for filing or discarding them.

3

THE FIRST RULE OF THUMB: *Answer business-related emails when you get them and delete unwanted junk mail liberally and quickly.*

Obviously, if an email is a coupon, or advertisement, DELETE. Otherwise, you can sort through emails a few different ways:[18]

- **Sort inbox by "from" rather than by date.** You will likely be able to batch-delete a number of unwanted messages while saving client-related emails for archival storage.

- **Sort inbox by "subject."** This will stack related messages together and connect them to other emails as part of a string.

- **Sort inbox in reverse date order.** The older the message, the less likely that it will be important, and the easier it will be to delete.

- **Remove yourself from one email list per day.**

---

18 https://www.mindtools.com/pages/article/managing-email.htms

- **If an email represents a task you need to complete, move it to your task folder.** Alternatively, you can create a to-do list and/ or action folders for it.

- **Investigate using third-party tools,** such as:
  - www.toodledo.com
  - www.rememberthemilk.com

- **Move appointments into your calendar** and store or discard appointment mail.

- **Move emails to an alternative folder for follow-up,** or convert this into a task for follow-up.

- **Keep only business email in your business email account.**

- **Don't clutter your email box with newsletters, subscriptions, shopping and shipping confirmations, etc. Instead, create a separate account for them using Gmail.**

- Don't allow emails to be a constant distraction. **Schedule a specific time to blast through your inbox** rather than obsessively checking them throughout the day.

- **Keep your email responses short.** Know when email is NOT the appropriate medium for communication. Pick up the phone or walk down the hall to see a colleague.

- **Create a system to automatically flag emails from specific people** so you can see them as soon as they arrive, such as key clients and contacts.

- **Activate case management software** to save incoming emails directly to a client's file.

- **If an email requires action, promptly forward it,** move it into a file folder, or refer it to your action list.

- **Set aside 30 minutes each week to clean out your emails.**

14
Assessing Your Finances

CASH FLOW

Entering solo practice can be a scary decision. After all, you're putting everything on the line and taking a chance on your ability to create and grow your own business. **CASH FLOW** will be one of your main concerns.

As we've seen, for solo law practitioners just starting out, working on a laptop from Starbucks may be cheap and convenient. In theory, all you really need is a computer, a printer, phone service, and access to a law library. But to represent clients and run a business properly, you must rent a real office 6-12 months after you launch your practice.

When it comes to outfitting your operation, it doesn't pay to pinch pennies.

You're going to need:

✓ An office

✓ Furniture

✓ Office supplies

✓ Support staff

So how much is this going to cost to create a practice? According to Sam Glover, the founder and editor-in-chief of Lawyerist, $3,000 is a starting point for the bare minimum, though $5,000 to $15,000 is more realistic.

It's obviously going to be dependent on **location**, your chosen **practice area**, the **level of your taste and choices**, and other variables.

Yes, it would be great to have a large office space and an interior designer to fill it, not to mention a complement of staff members too. But at the beginning, you can go with generic design choices and one legal assistant.

But no matter what, spending money is not optional.

Whether your initial capital investment comes from your own personal savings, loans from family and friends, credit cards, or a line of credit, you will need to establish a budget for your initial start-up.

It is critical to understand your:

- ✓ **Cash flow requirements**
- ✓ **Regular monthly expenses**
- ✓ **Potential sources of revenue**
- ✓ **Your living expenses until you begin to generate a reliable income**

Many solo lawyers starting out don't have savings or family resources, or a war chest of funds to get them through the start-up and/or tough times, so they will most likely have to finance or borrow the funds, paying them back as business flows into the practice.

To determine how much you need to open your practice and cover your overall expenses, factor in:

✓ **BUSINESS EXPENSES**

✓ **PERSONAL EXPENSES** (the money you'll need to survive while you're finding clients and networking).

✓ **ENOUGH SAVINGS FOR ONE YEAR** in order to lift the practice off the ground.

✓ **YOUR REPAYMENT OF DEBT** (loan deferments are often available, though you're still going to need some credit to begin the practice).

In order to get an overview of your entire financial picture, make an inventory of every expense in your PERSONAL LIFE:

3

- Automobile
- Child care
- Clothing
- Credit card fees
- Utilities
- Education
- Food
- Gifts (birthday, holiday, special occasions).
- Healthcare (primary, dental, medications).
- Household (rent, mortgage payment, maintenance and repairs, supplies).
- Insurance (automobile, health, life, disability, long-term care).
- Leisure (vacations, toys, books, magazines, movies, sporting events, memberships).
- Loans
- Pet care
- Transportation

Make an inventory of EVERY expense needed:

- Announcements, stationery, business cards, postage.
- First and last month's rent.
- Cost of office furniture, supplies, and modest decorating.
- Initial payment for telephone equipment, line charges and directory listings.
- Computer
- Printer
- Copy machine
- Student loan obligation (if you have one, try to extend or defer repayment).
- Investigator fees for personal injury cases
- Court filing fees for commencing litigation
- Electronic research or law books
- Rent
- Malpractice insurance

INSURANCE

Buying MALPRACTICE INSURANCE is essential for any law practice. The malpractice policies available in today's commercial market vary greatly, and insurance companies are more willing than ever to negotiate specific terms and conditions that address the unique risks faced by you and your firm.

Malpractice Insurance Protection

- **BUYING A POLICY IS MANDATORY. You need it from day one. Sure, some lawyers proceed without it, but it's a lot easier to sleep at night knowing you will be covered. Get the best, as opposed to the cheapest, insurance.**
- **Some state professional conduct rules require you to disclose**

the existence or nonexistence of malpractice insurance in your fee agreement.

- Your local bar association may have the best deal available.
- Should you ever change carriers, be sure that you do not have any gaps in your coverage.
- Attempt to get a policy that gives you the right to approve any settlements that are being made.
- BE AWARE OF THE DEDUCTIBLE
- BE AWARE OF ANY EXCLUSIONS
- New lawyers typically get the best deals because the insurance company wants you as a regular customer.
- Your starting rate will be lower because new lawyers don't have as many clients or legal matters.
- Fee arbitration and mediation clauses can reduce the risk of a malpractice claim.
- Review the cost of defense clause before purchasing, which could erode the coverage you thought you were buying, thereby encouraging early settlements of claims.
- If you practice in a law office suite, stipulate in your policy that you are NOT in partnership or responsible for any issues related to other lawyers.
- Consider paying a single premium, which covers you for all prior acts (known as tail coverage) if you decide to stop practicing law for a short or extended period of time.
- Consider purchasing umbrella (or excess) coverage, which picks up coverage where your primary policy ends.

Other Insurance Coverage:

- **PROPERTY** - Liability, wind, fire, earthquake, etc:
  - Replacement and cost of valuable papers

- Replacement value of office furniture
- Replacement of computers and data processor
- **WORKERS' COMPENSATION**
- **BUSINESS INTERRUPTION**
- **DISABILITY**
- **LIFE**
- **HEALTH PLAN**
- **CAR INSURANCE for business use:**
  - Non-owned automobile insurance in the event an employee uses your vehicle and damages it.
- **OFFICE BLOCK INSURANCE**
- **TRUST ACCOUNT THEFT**
- **ARBITRATOR or MEDIATOR insurance**
- **FIRE AND THEFT** (replacement-value clause verified).
- **NON-OWNED ASSETS insurance**

Memberships:

- The American Bar Association
- ABA Law Practice Management: www.lawpractice.org
- ABA solo and small firm and general practice division
- Local and state bar associations
- Your specific practice area associations

Continuing Legal Education (CLE) programs:

- The requirement varies by state, so check your state bar association for the specific requirement. Most states require 12-15 credits per year with 1-3 credits assigned to ethics.
- Practice management
- Timekeeping

- Practice area specific
- Ethics

General business training:

- A law practice is a business, so business training is critical to growing your firm and managing your clients.
- Marketing
- Finance
- Accounting
- Communications

Miscellaneous:

- Obtain city or county business licenses or permits.
- Order post office box (if needed).
  - Become a notary, or have someone on staff or close by who can act in that capacity .
  - Develop a disaster recovery plan for office, files, computers, etc.
  - Develop a plan for your illness, incapacity or death.

BORROWING FUNDS

Steps To Finding Your Financing Partner

It's highly suggested that you have **enough cash or a line of credit to cover start-up costs** and the first 6-12 months of operating expenses, plus personal living expenses:

- **SOURCES OF CREDIT:**
  - Local bank/credit union

☐   Personal, business loans

☐   Home equity, home refinance

☐   Line-of-credit to be drawn upon as needed

☐   Lease, equipment loans

☐   Family loans/private investor loans

☐   Personal savings

- **Can your spouse or partner earn enough income to support the family for the first year?**

- **Can you get a bank loan? Establish a relationship with your local banker.**

- **Can you procure a cosigner for the loan?**

- **Do you have a parent, in-law, or relative to lend you money or guarantee a bank loan?**

- **Could someone borrow the money for you? It may provide them with an interest deduction.**

- **Can you refinance your home, procuring enough cash to maintain your practice for a year?**

- **Can a friend or relative buy the equipment you need in his or her name and lease the equipment to you? This can provide a tax benefit to them.**

In order to approach any funding source, you're going to need a BUSINESS PLAN first. It must include:

✓ A company summary

✓ Proof of company ownership

✓ Start-up requirement summary

- Stationery
- Website creation

- Business internet
- Office equipment
- Rent
- Research and development
- Expensed equipment
- Other

✓ **Total Funding Required Summary:**
- Non-cash assets from start-up
- Current borrowing
- Long-term liabilities
- Accounts payable (outstanding bills)
- Other current liabilities

Although most banks have their own forms, it doesn't hurt to get a jump-start in exploring what information you will need:

- **PERSONAL INFORMATION**
  - Personal financial statement or net worth statement; a listing of assets and liabilities, plus additional detailed information.

- **PERSONAL TAX RETURNS (two years if available).**

- **Résumé or curriculum vitae—just to let your banker know a little more about you.**

- **BUSINESS INFORMATION**
  - Business balance sheet with assets and liabilities
  - Business tax returns
  - Business plan to inform your banker about your practice vision

- **FIND THE RIGHT PLACE WITHIN YOUR TARGET BANKS**
  - Banks vary in the areas that service law firms and attorneys. Make some calls to find out if business

banking, commercial banking, or private banking handles your potential relationship within a specific bank.

- Once you find a group that works with professionals, find out if there is someone who further specializes in attorneys.

- Set up a meeting and feel free to talk to several banks for your best fit.

- **DEVELOP A RELATIONSHIP AND PARTNERSHIP WITH YOUR NEW BANK**

  - Bankers prefer full relationships with clients, incorporating both checking and savings accounts, other deposits, and loans all in one place. Your relationship may also include Treasury Management as your practice grows with more complex needs.

- **YOUR BANKER IS YOUR PARTNER.** They want you to succeed, so don't hesitate to ask for their opinion. While you initially may be asking for service or structure on a loan, there may be a better way to achieve your financial goals. Remember, your banker has seen practices such as yours that may be further along. So he/she may have valuable feedback as to what has worked well and what has not.

Your banker can also be a business source for you, and vice versa. He/she may have other bank clients that ask for recommendations for attorneys, and you may have clients asking for a bank recommendation. It helps to understand what services and areas the bank may offer, and to let them know what your ideal client looks like.

Once you have your banking partner, it frees you to spend time on other aspects of developing your practice. Don't forget to check in periodically to give an update!

CREDIT CARDS

Use credit cards to finance your practice only as a last resort, when you have no alternative and cannot borrow the money from a relative or a bank (as interest rates are gouging, ranging from 15%-36%)

- **SHOP AROUND** for a card with the lowest interest rate and one with good points for cash rebates and redemption on flights, hotels, mileage, etc.
- **RETAIN MULTIPLE CREDIT CARDS,** in case you require fast cash.
- Always try to **PAY YOUR CREDIT CARD BILL IN FULL** (which can result in the bank providing a higher credit limit. You can also request a higher limit).
- **NEVER MISS A PAYMENT,** as it could lower your credit rating.
- Try to use each credit card every month so that you create an active status, which will further improve your credit rating.
- **NEVER USE ANY ONE CARD TO ITS MAXIMUM.**
- If you exceed your credit limit, this can cause forfeiture of the card or the lowering of your credit standing.
- **DO NOT MIX PERSONAL AND BUSINESS CHARGES** on the same credit card.
- Credit cards, which can be cancelled, are preferable to debit cards, which if lost or stolen, could be used to liquidate your bank account.

REMEMBER: *It may be cheaper to get a line of credit from a bank than paying interest on a credit card.*

SETTING UP YOUR FIRM'S BANK ACCOUNTS

As a solo practitioner, you're responsible for everything, from dealing with opposing counsel to the procurement of clients and staff, plus advertising and marketing too. So, it is best to:

✓ **Open, at a minimum, two accounts:**

- A business checking for day-to-day expense, with a minimum of $3,000-$5,000 for starters.

- An IOLTA trust account for client funds (not yours).

- Open a third account for excess revenue, i.e., your "rainy day" account, as a safety net for months when your income falls short of meeting expenses.

- Open a fourth account for payment of taxes (make sure this reserve doesn't get spent).

✓ **Pay estimated taxes or take a penalty and write a bigger check at year's end.**

✓ **Consider using a payroll service to pay yourself, which will withhold and pay taxes.**

✓ **Establish a system for accepting electronic payments, e.g., credit card payments and bank transfers:**

- QuickBooks
- PayPal
- Square
- LawPay
- Your bank

Before you begin using one of the services listed above, consult your state's professional conduct rules regarding electronic payments. There may be restrictions regarding which bank account you can use to accept payments.

✓ **Safety deposit box**

15
Choosing Your Form of Entity

While your thoughts may be predominantly focused on where to set up your practice and how to furnish and staff it, there's one primary decision you have to make in advance in opening your own law firm.

Which type of legal entity you will form?

Whether it's a PC, LLC, Subchapter S Corp, partnership, or sole proprietorship, there are pluses and minuses relevant to:

- ✓ Liability protection
- ✓ Tax treatment
- ✓ Ease of operation

A menu of possibilities is listed below, but my recommendation is to **CONSULT WITH AN EXPERIENCED ACCOUNTANT OR TAX ATTORNEY** *who can advise you on which entity to choose.*

Your decision will be based upon:

- ▪ Assets and income
- ▪ Size and location of your firm
- ▪ Your long-term goals and areas of practice
- ▪ Taxation

- Liability
- Succession/dissolution

Here are the choices based upon the main categories defined by the American Bar Association:[19]

- **CORPORATIONS:** Becoming a professional corporation (PC) requires having shareholders, a board of directors, and a management team, all operating separately from one another. As a sole owner, you can only be one shareholder, or one board member, each role separate, and you have to keep careful records to remain in compliance with state law, or risk losing the limited liability advantage gained by maintaining the business as a separate legal entity. Corporations also have to maintain minutes for board meetings and file an annual report in most states.

  - **The upside:** The separation between ownership and management creates a barrier to protect the corporation owner from liability.

  - **The downside:** The profits of the company are taxed at the corporate tax rate before being distributed to shareholders, who are subsequently liable for taxes on corporate gains, creating "double taxation." All in all, structuring a new practice by creating a corporation is not recommended.

- **LIMITED LIABILITY COMPANIES:** Unincorporated LLC (or PLLC—Professional Limited Liability Company) is a business structure that combines the limited personal liability feature of a corporation with the single taxation feature of a sole proprietorship firm. Taxes are recorded directly on the sole member's tax returns.

---

19 http://www.americanbar.org/publications/tyl/topics/solo-small-firm/law-firm-choice-entity.html

- **The upside:** It gives you the perk of pass-through taxes, limited liability, and legal protection for your personal assets. The tax structure of an LLC is more advantageous than that of the professional corporation. Tax returns for an LLC are filed with the taxation authorities only for the purpose of information, and each shareholder files a tax return separately. To maintain its limited liability status, it must file paperwork with the state and maintain separate books, records, and bank accounts from its members.

- **The downside:** Where the operating agreement is silent, LLCs are governed by statute. This may lead to unanticipated or unwanted results in situations such as distributions or dissolutions.

- **SUBCHAPTER S CORPORATIONS:** This is strictly a tax decision that can be made whether or not you're a corporation or an LLC.

  - **The upside:** There is no corporate level taxation, which can yield very high tax savings, since corporations do not generally pay any federal income tax. Instead, the corporation's income or losses are divided among and passed through to its shareholders who must then report the income or loss on their own individual income tax returns.

  - **The downside:** S corporations are limited in their use, as your firm must be a domestic company… it must have only non-business, non-foreign owners, have fewer than 100 owners, and have only one classification of stock. For most solo practitioners, none of these factors would be deterrents.

▪ PARTNERSHIPS:

- **A GENERAL PARTNERSHIP** is an unincorporated entity that typically has limited or no filing requirements with the state. Unlike the corporation or the LLC, a general partnership does not protect its owners from personal liability, meaning that each partner could be responsible for every debt the general partnership accrues.

- **LIMITED PARTNERSHIPS (LPs)** differ from general partnerships in that typically only one partner needs to be responsible for the debts of the company. The remaining partners can be limited partners, who cannot be held liable for any debts. Some states require that a limited partner cannot have any meaningful control over the company.

- **LIMITED LIABILITY PARTNERSHIPS (LLPs)** are also partnerships that afford limited liability protection to the limited partners. In some states, all partners are afforded this protection, just like an LLC.

  - ☐ The protections and availability of LPs and LLPs vary significantly between states, so it is important to check local laws regarding these entities before forming either of them. LPs and LLPs have more formalities and filing requirements than a general partnership.

  - ☐ General partnerships, LPs, and LLPs are taxed as pass-through entities. In this type of taxation, the company will issue K-1s to the partners, and those partners will record that income on their personal tax returns.

■ **SOLE PROPRIETORSHIPS:** These are unincorporated entities that cost nothing to establish and require little or no filing with the state government. A sole proprietorship can have only one member, and is taxed as a disregarded entity, meaning that all profits and losses are recorded on the owner's tax return. Whereas the formulation of an LLC allows liability protection, the owner of the sole proprietorship can be held 100 percent liable for the actions of the company and of any employee of the company. This is NOT recommended for the solo lawyer.

■ **C CORPORATIONS:** Refers to any corporation that is taxed separately from its owners, and is distinguished from an S corporation, which generally is not taxed separately. This type of corporation provides several non-tax benefits (such as limited liability for the owners), and is popular as a staging base for raising large amounts of investment capital by going public. Unlike an S corporation, however, the entity's income is taxed twice, first as corporate income, then as shareholder (dividend) income.

■ **PARTNERSHIP AGREEMENTS** (should you take one in):

- Capital/equity from partners
- Withdrawal/retirement issues
- Compensation and profit distribution
- Each partner's role in the practice:
  - ☐ Managing partner
  - ☐ Rainmaker
  - ☐ Others

■ ACCOUNTING NEEDS

- Consult with CPA on procedures for:
  - ☐ Chart of accounts
  - ☐ Profit and loss statements
  - ☐ Balance sheets
  - ☐ Cash flow statement:
    - ◆ Quarterly and annual tax returns
    - ◆ Payroll services
    - ◆ Bank and trust accounting systems
    - ◆ Software compatible with accountant's

For more tips and downloadable resources, visit the Ironman Resource Page, at www.PracticeLawLikeAnIronman.com/resources

PART FOUR

THE CLOCK IS TICKING

16
Keeping Clients Satisfied and Managing Fees

"You can buy a person's time; you can buy their physical presence...but you cannot buy enthusiasm or loyalty, or devotion of hearts, minds, or souls. You must earn these."

– Clarence Francis, Former Chairman of General Foods Corporation

Now that your firm's funding is established and office mechanics are up and running, the next piece of the puzzle is perfecting the art of client services. This includes how clients are treated in and out of the office, and how your office manages its time, billing, and fees.

Serving the client by adding value is the best way to expand any practice. **Your motto is: I GIVE because it's who I am and what I do.** The end result is that you get rave reviews and testimonials that exponentially expand your business.

My wish is always to:

- Have happy clients who want to refer me business.
- Have a happy staff that receives consistent raises and bonuses.
- Have a happy family due to the fruits of my labor.
- Have the best criminal, DUI/family law firm in my region.
- Have no worries about being able to make payroll and monthly bills.
- Put away money in investments for retirement.

120

- Grow the business and hire attorneys, paralegals and support staff.
- Celebrate great outcomes with my staff, creating a clap, clap, clap vibe.
- Leave a legacy of impeccable ethics.
- Stay on the cutting edge of my area of practice.

Client Satisfaction Checklist

- ✓ Do you keep clients scrupulously up-to-date on their cases?
- ✓ Do you inform clients about changes in the law pertinent to them?
- ✓ Do you return phone calls promptly?
- ✓ Do you establish a personal bond with clients, showing interest in their lives?
- ✓ Do you invite them to meals and sporting events or social events?
- ✓ Do you acknowledge birthdays and anniversaries?
- ✓ Do you visit their place of business?
- ✓ When concluding representation, do you write a closing letter?
- ✓ Do you use technology to provide excellent service?
- ✓ Do you use a client survey to assess client satisfaction? More on this later.
- ✓ Are you asking clients to refer their friends and colleagues?

For a moment, let's now circle back to something we talked about earlier in the book: the **POWER OF VISUALIZATION.**

Write down a script of what you imagine to be the perfect experience for a new client coming into your office. Envision the scene in all its detail, from the moment they drive into the parking lot and walk into the lobby or reception area of your office, to the moment they leave.

Visualize your perfect office

- What do they see?
- What do they hear?
- How do they feel?
- What kind of greeting do they receive from your employees?
- How is the staff dressed?
- How does the support staff comport themselves?
- Do you offer coffee or tea? Water or soft drinks? On a silver platter?
- Where does the client sit? Where do you sit?
- Are they able to hear staff operations and conversation?
- What does your office look like?
- How is the lighting?
- Do you take calls or staff interruptions during the meeting? You should not, unless it's an emergency. Give your client your undivided attention.
- How do you end the meeting?
- Do you walk the client back to the lobby?
- How do you say good-bye?

For additional resources that will facilitate the planning of your practice as well as your implementation process, visit the Ironman Resource page, www.PracticeLawLikeAnIronman.com/resources

Encourage employees to visualize this scene too, and provide them with a script of how you want this experience to play out, which will ensure a consistent performance.

The script or system spells out each employee's:

- Words
- Appearance
- Demeanor
  - Being relentless about details
  - Surprising clients with something extra
  - Leaving a lasting impression as clients depart the office
  - Walking clients to the door and thanking them

4

REMEMBER...*the greeting your clients receive when they walk into your office is crucial. That first impression really counts. You don't want a painfully shy person at the front reception desk. As we discussed earlier, you need someone who is friendly, warm, engaging, and outgoing. A little wit doesn't hurt either!*

The caller or visitor will be paying attention to your staff's verbal cues and tone, just as much as their words. Never make a potential client feel like they are interrupting your day because you have to answer a telephone or look up from your desk.

Give each employee a copy of the book *Creating Magic: 10 Common Sense Leadership Strategies from a Life at Disney* by Lee Cockerell. And have office employees involved in creating and revising the practice protocol:

- Answering the door.
- Answering the telephone (more on this later).
- Interacting with clients in the lobby or reception room.
- Maintaining proper eye contact and body language (convey friendliness and patience; inspire trust).
- Dealing with obnoxious clients patiently! The more agitated they get, the calmer and quieter the staff gets.
- Not taking anything a client says personally.
- Cultivating the art of apologizing when needed (don't blame, don't explain, make it brief and to the point).

■ **Consider creating a video for teaching purposes.**

■ **Include scripts for both in-person visits and phone protocol.**

■ **List all potential conflicts for client/employee interactions, such as:**

- Inquiries about a bill
- Inquiries about the status of a case
- Complaints about customer service

You'll find that your established system for interacting with clients, *i.e., your hospitality protocol,* is the "secret sauce" of your law practice, assuring customer satisfaction.

It's going to be a smoothly operating machine. So even if you don't happen to be in the office, an agreed-upon system for interacting with clients permits your business to run on automatic, drivable by others, should you not be available.

In most law practices, interaction with clients all begins with answering the phone, which is one of the most important functions in any office.

The greeting a caller gets from your receptionist is the firm's welcome mat. It's designed to provide efficient, smart access to any and all information or update on their case or concern as needed.

- Don't rush
- Be empathetic
- Be efficient
- Take notes
- Have a script ready for any contingency

In my own office, my legal secretary, Jen, or my client intake specialist Amy, can often be heard saying:

"Ed, I think you have made a smart choice in calling us today. Mr. Adams has years of experience handling exactly this type of case. He has handled literally hundreds of such cases with a proven track record of getting outstanding outcomes for his clients. I'm confident he can help you with your issue. Would you like to set up an appointment with Mr. Adams? He charges $200 for a 30 minute consultation and $350 for a 60 minute consultation. Should you decide to hire him, this will be credited toward your initial fee."

NOTE: Charging for an initial consultation will steer away the tire kickers and other people merely trying to pick your brain for free information or advice with no intention to hire you.

17
Keep-a-Client-Happy Tips and Client Management

✓ **RETURN CLIENT CALLS** within three hours, or have a staff member do it, or inform clients of your general availability via phone.

✓ **BE RECEPTIVE**, returning calls on weeknights and weekends if required.

✓ Provide your **PERSONAL CELL PHONE NUMBER** to clients.

✓ For potential clients, **ADVISE** them of attorney-client privilege.

✓ On any case, **ASK: WHAT, WHERE, WHEN, WHY, HOW, WHO?**

✓ **CREATE AN ELECTRONIC INTAKE FORM** that includes slots for witnesses, investigator and police data, etc.

✓ Create a **PROFESSIONAL WELCOMING GREETING** for phone reception, including proper screening of callers.

✓ **FOR ESTABLISHED CLIENTS,** access their complete records on the computer as you're taking the call, including memos and correspondence, pleadings, discovery, trial documents, etc. This should all be at your fingertips:

  • Use a fully-featured document management software system to allow a rapid search and indexing of client and court files.

- The program must be server or cloud-based.
- It must integrate with scanning and email programs to store documents created outside of the system.
- It must include different versions of a document, and link clients and matters in documents.
- You must be able to see what work has been done for clients across multiple files.
- The program should have calendar features that allow your staff to view and schedule deadlines and appointments.

✓ **SYSTEMATIZE** a detailed message-taking protocol that outlines the issue, its urgency, and a promise to return the call promptly.

✓ After lengthy telephone calls, **DICTATE A SUMMARY MEMORANDUM.**

✓ If you **DECLINE** representation, follow up with a referral.

✓ **USE A SPEAKERPHONE** or telephone headset to keep hands free for note-taking during a call.

✓ **HIRE AN OUTSIDE ANSWERING SERVICE** to receive overnight calls, training them in the way you want your calls answered.

✓ **IF YOU CAN'T AFFORD A RECEPTIONIST DURING DAYTIME HOURS TO ANSWER THE PHONE, CREATE A FANTASTIC VOICEMAIL**—short and to the point—and provide your cell number for instant access.

4

And don't forget, as your firm's leader-in-chief, it's your role to provide:

- **INSPIRATION** – your ability to make someone want to work with you and accomplish their goal.

- **INNOVATION** – your take on your law specialty, finding a way to shake up your industry.

- **PLAY** – making your business one that's fun to work in and fun to do business with, using humor as a powerful tool rather than being dry and fact-based.

- **COMMUNITY** – creating a dialogue and connection to your city or neighborhood, becoming part of it by contributing to it.

- **CONVENIENCE** – being fully accessible rather than walled off from the public, effectively using both direct phone contact and social media to enhance client relationships, knowing that people pay more for a convenient experience.

- **SIMPLICITY** – the most appreciated attribute, allowing clients to clearly understand the services you provide via marketing and social media. Clarity is king.

- **SURPRISE** – exceeding a client's expectations and providing something they never guessed. Who doesn't like to receive unexpected gifts, overnight packages, and handwritten notes?

Secrets to keeping your clients satisfied

- ✓ Keep your promises
- ✓ Assess their needs and expectations
- ✓ Send alerts/updates/newsletters/E- books
- ✓ Send birthday greetings
- ✓ Introduce clients to key colleagues

✓ Provide clients with access to important events

✓ Assist in improving client profitability via value-added legal services

✓ Be proactive in planning legal strategies

✓ Offer targeted seminars

✓ Personalize the follow-up and be shareable:

- Phone
- Email
- Social media
- Gather together like-minded clients

✓ Take small groups to lunch

✓ Listen to what your clients are saying without interrupting

✓ Demonstrate empathy and compassion to cement a friendship

✓ Allow them to see you as a person and vice-versa

✓ Communicate with them about things other than law:

- Hobbies
- Vacations
- Funny incidents
- Their family pet

✓ Give them the VIP treatment:

- Serve clients with a friendly, polite, appealing, and kind attitude.
- Avoid the word NO. It's a discouraging response that translates as lack of effort. Instead, replace no with NO PROBLEM.

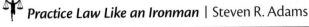

- Return all phone calls and emails promptly.
- Take time to write handwritten notes.
- Serve with consistency, integrity, creativity, and sincerity.
- Pay attention to both legal and non-legal aspects (a client's stress level, personal concerns—in other words, the full picture).
- Serve new clients by presenting them with the firm's kit for orientation:
  - ☐ What to expect from your practice
  - ☐ How to contact anyone in your practice
  - ☐ Data needed from the client to get started
  - ☐ A copy of the retainer agreement
  - ☐ A copy of your newsletter and recent published articles
  - ☐ Testimonials
  - ☐ Client Satisfaction Survey (see below).
- **Serve new clients by doing your homework:**
  - ☐ Request background case documents if available
  - ☐ Research lawyers or investigators with whom the client has discussed the case prior to you
- **Serve clients by soliciting their online feedback:**
  - ☐ Ask them to rate your business on a scale of 1 to 10.
  - ☐ If score is 1 to 4, client should be directed to a page that apologizes and notifies that client will receive an immediate phone call.
  - ☐ If it's 5 to 7, send the client to a page that says you are not happy until they are more satisfied, and ask what you could do better.

- ☐ For the 8 to 10 score, redirect them to a form that allows them to submit a testimonial.
- ☐ Use Wufoo or Formstack to run this process.
- ☐ Host a client appreciation event annually.
- ☐ Hire video crew, distributing it as a keepsake.
- ☐ Film testimonials if client consents to it.
- ☐ Include anecdotal accounts from clients about their experiences.
- ☐ Develop exit interviews for outgoing clients.

- **Create a Client Satisfaction Survey (as below, a fantastic list compiled by Lawyers Mutual Liability Insurance Company of North Carolina):**
  - ☐ How did you hear about our firm?
  - ☐ If by referral, who sent you?
  - ☐ If by advertisement, which one?
  - ☐ What do you think of our advertising and marketing efforts?
  - ☐ How easy was it to schedule an appointment?
  - ☐ Were you treated well in your initial visit?
    - ◆ What made you decide to hire us?
    - ◆ This is the true differentiator
    - ◆ Make it the core marketing message for your business
  - ☐ Did we complete your work on time?
  - ☐ Did we meet your expectations?
  - ☐ Did we communicate regularly?
  - ☐ Do you feel we listened to you?
  - ☐ Did we return your phone calls promptly?

- ☐ Did we keep you informed about developments in your case?
- ☐ Were you treated with courtesy and respect?
- ☐ Was our staff helpful?
- ☐ What's the one thing we do better than anyone else?
- ☐ Do you feel we understood your problem?
- ☐ Did we lay out options and explain the pros and cons of each?
- ☐ Did we come up with creative solutions?
- ☐ Did we adequately explain our fee and billing procedures?
- ☐ Were our bills clear and understandable?
- ☐ Was our total fee fair?
- ☐ Were you satisfied with the case outcome? Why or why not?
- ☐ Would you come back to us for legal help? Why or why not?
- ☐ Would you recommend us to others? Why or why not?
- ☐ Would you like to be placed on our mailing list?
- ☐ Have you visited our website? What are your impressions?
- ☐ Have you read our blog? Your impressions?
- ☐ Do you read our newsletter? Do you find it helpful?

4

Client Relationship Management Data

- Compile Client Relationship Management data (CRM), used to manage and analyze customer interactions with the goal of:
  - Improving business relationships
  - Assisting in customer retention
  - Driving new business forward
    - CRM software programs offer training and customization, tracking every interaction with a client or prospect, and include:
      - ACT
      - Goldmine
      - LawRuler
      - Maximizer
      - Salesforce.com
      - Sunrise
      - Pipedrive
      - Marketing 360
      - Accelo
      - Nutshell
      - Insightly
      - Zoho
    - These programs also:
      - Track appointments
      - Track phone calls
      - Track court dates
      - Track social engagements
      - Track marketing effectiveness
      - Track sales force automation
      - Track customer service

4

- **Written communication with clients (have templates ready to go):**
  - ☐ Engagement letter
  - ☐ Notices regarding court dates
  - ☐ Hearing date letters
  - ☐ Trial date letters
  - ☐ Deposition date letters
  - ☐ Deadline date letters
  - ☐ Time-triggered letters for some future legal need of the client.
  - ☐ Work product letters (cover page with enclosed work product).
  - ☐ For Your Information letters (an interesting case that client may be interested in).
  - ☐ A closing or disengagement letter
- **A survey letter at the end of the case to summarize its essentials.**
- **Practice reflective listening—reiterate or paraphrase what he or she said.**
  - ☐ What brings our customers joy?
  - ☐ What are they worried about?
  - ☐ What challenges do they face?
  - ☐ What goals are they striving to attain?
  - ☐ What experience thrills them?
  - ☐ Where do they get their information?
  - ☐ Whom do they trust most?
- **Analyze potential referral possibilities:**
  - ☐ What additional legal services will each client likely need?

☐ What colleagues, organizations or centers of influence could a client introduce you to for referrals?

    ☐ Keep in touch: Send updates on the law, newsletters, birthday, anniversary, holiday cards and invitations to social events.

- **Client matter endings:**

    ☐ Celebrate a good outcome with your client.

    ☐ Answer final questions about the resolution of the matter.

    ☐ Ask your client about their plans for the future.

    ☐ Let them know you want to work with them again.

    ☐ Ask them to keep you in mind for a referral.

    ☐ Ask them to write a testimonial, which will be posted on your website and on Avvo, Google, Facebook, Yelp, etc... all of it included in your practice literature.

4

Knowing When And How to Say No

As Jay G. Foonberg wisely advises in his book, *How to Start & Build a Law Practice:*

- ▪ **Tell a potential client the truth:**
  - No merit to the case
  - Uneconomical prospect

- ▪ **Suggest alternatives:**
  - Small claims court
  - Legal aid
  - Public defenders
  - Bar Association lawyer referral system

- Alternative dispute resolution
- Consumer advocate offices

■ **Put your decision in writing after you decline the case.**

■ **Create a "prospective clients" file and put a copy of that letter and any handwritten notes into that file.**

■ **When you can and can't withdraw from a case (refer to your state code of professional conduct first, or your state disciplinary code):**

- Leave early in the case when you are not getting paid.
- Leave when you will be called as a witness in the case.
- Leave when you have a conflict of interest with another client (easily accomplished with a conflict check before accepting the case).
- Say no when you're not competent to handle the matter.
- Leave when the client offered forged or perjured testimony on material issues (withdrawal may be mandatory).
- Leave if a case has no merit or is only being maintained for delay or harassment.
- Say no when your participation would be illegal, or prohibited under disciplinary rules.
- Leave when you're fired!
- Don't leave when:
  - ☐ The client has already paid your fee in full, unless you wish to refund the total and turn his or her file over to the client or to another counselor.
  - ☐ It prejudices your client's case.

- **CLIENTS TO AVOID, as described by Brian Tannebaum in his book** *The Practice: Brutal Truths About Lawyers and Lawyering:*
  - Incessant name droppers who want a discount.
  - Chronic re-schedulers.
  - Prospects that say "money is not a problem."
  - Prospective clients with a lawyer in another state that wants to call the shots.
  - Prospective clients that want to review the work that they have done on the case and have you proofread their documents.
  - Clients who have fired their first, second, or third lawyer and now want to hire you.
  - Any prospective client seeking a free, detailed analysis of their issue.
- **FIRED AS A LAWYER—DAMAGE CONTROL:**
  - Remain calm and detached.
  - Don't take the termination personally.
  - Efficiently make the client's files available.
  - Send by certified mail a letter to your client containing the following information, as summarized by Jay Foonberg's book *How to Start & Build A Law Practice*:
    - ☐ Confirm that you are no longer the lawyer.
    - ☐ Inform the client that you are returning all original documents and keeping copies for your file.
    - ☐ Inform the client of your service fees, if any, for providing all files.
    - ☐ Ask permission to destroy whatever documents you do not wish to store.

4

- ☐ Cite a date from which to measure all possible statutes of limitation in case a client later wants to sue you for malpractice.

- ☐ Assert that if the next lawyer loses the case or produces an unfavorable result, you are not accepting responsibility.

- ☐ Set the record straight about fee disputes, if any, that arose after the person was no longer a client.

- ☐ Let the client know that you expect to be paid immediately for any fees due. If there is a dispute, offer arbitration or mediation.

- ☐ Never shut the door for good, as a client may return.

- ☐ Keep meticulous notes after being terminated. The services rendered during the representation will most likely not be privileged, but what you did after the representation may be privileged if it was in anticipation of litigation.

18
The Meter is Running

A key part of your effectiveness as a solo or small firm is, undoubtedly, your wise use of TIME. In fact: **There is nothing more important to lawyers than time, as we base our entire livelihoods on it.** We live on a deadline. And we bill, one way or another, based upon the expenditure of our time.

So how you allocate and manage the hours of the day will dramatically affect the success of your practice. This is particularly true since you're wearing multiple hats—as attorney, networker, marketer, office manager, and chief financial officer.

Before we get into the issue of billing, here are some overall tips for maximizing smart use of your time, as summarized in *How to Do More in Less Time: The Complete Guide to Increasing Your Productivity and Improving Your Bottom Line,* by Allison C. Shields and Daniel J. Siegel:

- **Before leaving the office at the end of the work day:**
    - Review your time (records) sheet, and prepare a new one.
    - Prepare a list of to-do's and appointments for the next day.
    - Prioritize tasks in terms of importance and deadlines:
        - Block-out the number of hours needed for prioritized work, and do not take calls or have meetings unless there is true urgency.
    - Email your schedule to your secretary before leaving.
    - List three goals for the next day's work.
    - Once weekly, create a preset plan of action for the following week.

- If a new matter arises, add it to the bottom of the list.
- Be flexible: Your schedule is not set in stone:
  - ☐ Recognize that there will be last-minute emergencies, unforeseen circumstances, or a client crisis that must be addressed.
  - ☐ Be sure to include marketing, management, administration, business development and client work into your schedule each week.

- **DISCIPLINE YOURSELF to maintain your agenda, which allows you to be in control of your time:**
  - Say no to interruptions
    - ☐ Create a "Do Not Disturb" time in your office, uninterrupted time to work on Special projects
    - ☐ Marketing plans
    - ☐ Staff training
    - ☐ Learning something new that will help grow the business
  - Eliminate distractions:
    - ☐ Do **not** multitask, as switching back and forth between tasks costs you time. It can take up to 15 minutes to return to full function on a complex task.
    - ☐ Keep your door closed to limit coworker interruption.
    - ☐ Train staff to screen calls, or use an answering service.
    - ☐ Don't interrupt staff focused on their own tasks.
    - ☐ Reserve a pocket of time for accumulated staff queries.
    - ☐ Do not engage in shopping online.

- ☐ Limit how often you check incoming email (the average person checks their email 15 times daily).
- ☐ Manage your technology—don't let it manage you.
- ☐ Avoid web surfing.
- ☐ Don't stretch coffee breaks.
- ☐ Limit personal phone calls.
- ☐ For callbacks from clients, let them know when you're available to talk.
- ☐ Cultivate the ability to say no.

- **SCHEDULE RELAXATION TIME** with family and friends for recreation and socialization.

- **START EARLY.** If you're an early riser (as I am), you can accomplish a great deal between 3:30 am and 8 am, before a "normal" business day starts. The advantages:
  - ☐ You can prepare, prioritize, think, read, and write
  - ☐ No staff interruptions
  - ☐ No phone calls
  - ☐ No emails
  - ☐ No faxes
  - ☐ No messengers

- **DELEGATE EFFECTIVELY.** At least 50 percent of what needs to be communicated to clients is or should be delegated to the paralegals and office staff that can do everything that is not attorney-dependent.

- **CREATE A DETAILED TIME LOG FOR ONE WEEK** — both work and personal — to analyze how you're spending your time (and encourage your staff to do the same). This exercise will help you better manage your future time and reveal how much time is wasted.

4

- Once you've collected the data over the course of a week, **sort it into general categories,** as described in *The E-myth Attorney: Why Most Legal Practices Don't Work and What to Do about It* by Michael Gerber and Robert Armstrong:

  ☐ Client meetings

  ☐ Document preparation

  ☐ Managing email

  ☐ Web surfing

  ☐ Phone calls

  ☐ Administrative tasks

  ☐ Marketing

  ☐ Research

  ☐ Eating

  ☐ Spending time with your family

  ☐ Attending meetings

  ☐ Playing with your kids

  ☐ Yes, even going to the restroom

  ☐ Sleeping[20]

    ◆ Calculate the percentage of time you spend in each activity.
    ◆ Determine tasks for delegation, focusing on your strengths.
    ◆ Reduce interruptions.
    ◆ Schedule a succinct staff meeting weekly (and standup conferences with key staff periodically) to increase productivity.

---

20 *E-Myth Attorney: Why Most Law Practices Don't Work and What To Do About It*, by Michael E. Gerber, Robert Armstrong, and Sanford M. Fisch

What To Charge Clients

Some lawyers setting out on a solo practice say that there's no more-loathed task than keeping track of billing time. Writing down every moment of your legal time spent, in six-minute increments, can be a burdensome task for any lawyer, especially one in private practice.

If you were accustomed to having a salaried position at the DA's office (as I was), or at a government bureau or corporate firm, timekeeping was a non-issue. But now that you're on your own, assigning the value of your time is a mandatory task that must be handled efficiently. **Rule #1: Do not negotiate your fee.** When a prospective client tells you that Lawyer Smith is willing to do the same work for $2,000 less, tell the person kindly that he can then hire Lawyer Smith.

Billing protocols, as listed below, vary widely, depending upon your area of practice and the mix of cases. For sure, a solo or small firm may utilize more than one billing format, depending on the case, per the options summarized in James A. Durham and Deborah McMurray's *The Lawyer's Guide to Marketing Your Practice:*

4

- **FIXED FEES, THE BILLABLE HOUR, BY THE HOUR (MOST TYPICAL):**
    - Be competitive in your area of practice.
    - Be competitive in your geographical area.
    - Consider a blended hourly rate (work delegated to an associate or lowest-cost provider).
    - Never take a case for less than 10 hours upfront.
    - Rather than using legal software, some lawyers still prefer using an old-school tracking form, whether jotted down or typed:
        - ☐ Client
        - ☐ Matter

☐ Time

☐ Description of work

- Keep a printout of the time conversions so you don't have to keep doing the math:

  ☐ .1 = 6 minutes

  ☐ .2 = 12 minutes

  ☐ .9 = 54 minutes

- **FLAT FEES, known as Lump Sum Fee:**

  - Client knows fee at the outset, not based on time.

  - Allows client to budget and avoid billing surprises.

  - Lawyer assumes risk for cost overruns.

  - Lawyer foresees all contingencies.

  - Client assumes risk for an undesirable outcome.

  - When flat fee exhausted, morale and enthusiasm may wane.

  - Flat fee can include a provision that allows both client and attorney to revise the flat fee agreement should an unforeseen circumstance occur.

- **CONTINGENCY FEES, based upon a favorable result, i.e., the amount of money a lawyer recovers in a settlement or court award, usually a percentage of the damages awarded in favor of your client:**

  - Vary widely from state to state/lawyer to lawyer, and maximums may be set by statute.

  - Based on total amount recovered, net of expenses.

  - The standard is 33 1/3 percent for pre-trial settlement, and 40 percent if the case goes to trial.

  - Some states allow a sliding scale with higher contingencies for lower recovery.

- **PRO BONO**
  - Provides opportunity to get court experience.
  - Provides opportunity to know the judges.
  - Paves the way for future paying clients.
  - May allow the award of attorney fees, depending on the case.
  - Your retainer agreement should reserve the right to withdraw your representation if withdrawal is permitted by the Rules of Professional Conduct.

- **REFERRAL FEES (sometimes prohibited under state codes):**
  - Allows you to share the work and share the fees if permitted in your jurisdiction.
  - Client must consent to a division of fees.
  - Client cannot be overcharged to cover the fee splitting.
  - Unless each lawyer assumes joint responsibility for the representation, the fee must be shared proportional to the services performed.
  - Referral fees cannot be paid to a non-lawyer for referring clients.
  - Consult your state's rules of professional conduct for specific requirements and restrictions on referral fees.

- **RETAINER FEES, a down payment against future costs to be billed, placed in a trust account with cost of services deducted from that account as they accrue:**
  - A written retainer agreement is mandatory.
  - Lawyer gets a monetary advance to avoid collection issues.
  - Balance must be kept current to accurately reflect ongoing costs.
  - Must clearly specify what the retainer agreement covers.

4

- If you get fired early on, you must return the percentage of the fee that has not yet been earned.
- Inform the client that you report all cash payments to the IRS.
- Do not accept large cash fees of $10,000 or more.

- **STATUTORY FEES,** set by statute or court in probate, bankruptcy, or other proceedings.

- **BONUS FEES:** Check state bar rules related to bonus fees:
  - Performance bonus based upon results

- **HYBRID FEES:** combines flat fee with a bonus:
  - May combine elements of contingency and hourly (or flat) fee agreements. The contingency fee involves an element of risk and heightens the case screening process such that only cases likely to be winners are acceptable. Following a hybrid structure, the attorney charges a reduced rate to work the case and is rewarded by a bonus contingent on a positive outcome.
  - Allows handling of cases with lower probability of success, which facilitates justice to a greater number of clients.
  - Guarantees income upfront.
  - Total fee must still be reasonable.

- **VOLUME DISCOUNTS/DISCOUNTED FEES** (not usually advised):
  - Used for high-volume routine matters
  - Provides guaranteed work for law firm
  - Reduced rates give client more incentive for repeat business
    Diminishes brand
  - Creates resentment from other clients

The bill-per-hour is still the most widely accepted way for an attorney to charge a client, though you have many other options as well.

- What will your billable hour be?
- What will your flat fee be?
- How does your fee structure vary according to your area(s) of practice?
- How much money do you expect to generate each month? For the year?
- What will you do to increase your hourly rates?
- What will you do to become more time efficient?
- What will you do to delegate your work?
- How much time a year will you spend on pro bono work?

4

19

Retainer Agreements, Engagment Letters, and Easy Payment

Regardless of what fee structure you employ, **a key part of client relations is directly defining your firm's payment policies.** So at the initial consultation, you must have a detailed conversation about:[21]

✓ **Retainer agreement/engagement letter**[22]

- Define the scope of goals and services[23]

- Clarify the amount of time needed to achieve results

- Estimate the fees or disbursements that the client will likely incur

- Define the fee structure

- Confirm the monetary retainer

- Clarify additional fees the client may be responsible for (e.g. expert witness fees, financial valuations, etc.).

- Cite the rate of interest that will be charged on delinquent accounts and when accounts become delinquent.

- Outline the consequences of the client's failure to pay.

- Attach the lawyer or paralegal's billing policy

- Describe the manner of communication between lawyer and client (e.g. telephone, email, mail, fax).

---

21 http://www.americanbar.org/content/dam/aba/administrative/labor_law/meetings/2010/2010_ethics_jarvis.authcheckdam.pdf
22 http://www.lsuc.on.ca/RetainerAgreementOrEngagementLetter/
23 *The Practice* by Brian Tannebaum

- Define estimated time that it will normally take for the lawyer or paralegal to respond to client calls, emails, letters or other communications.

- Define the terms of lawyer withdrawal from representation (e.g. client's failure to pay retainers or accounts in accordance with the retainer agreement, any other circumstances contemplated by the Lawyers Rules of Professional Conduct or the Paralegal Rules of Conduct).

- Define ownership of file contents

- Define charges for file transfer

- Define scope of the engagement (particularly important if work undertaken for a fixed fee).

- Specify the goals of the engagement

- Specify who will work on the case

- Identify favored methods of communication

Visit the Ironman resource page, at www.PracticeLawLikeAnIronman.com/resources for additional resources and tips to help jump-start your own solo or small practice.

✓ **Explain how your firm's fee is calculated**

- Be specific in fee agreements, as any ambiguity will result in a judgment against a lawyer who prepared it.

✓ **Offer payment convenience**

- Accept credit cards by phone.

- Use your smartphone or tablet as a credit card machine.

- As back-up, consider asking client for a third-party guarantor or cosigner.

✓ **Credit Cards and Electronic Payments**

- **QUICKBOOKS:** If you're already using QuickBooks, activate QuickBooks Services for receiving credit cards. ($19.95 monthly fee plus a fee for each transaction: 1.64 percent plus 27 cents for a swiped card; 2.47 percent plus 27 cents for a keyed card).

- **PAYPAL:** Easily set up with your email address and a bank account number. No monthly fees. You only pay for each transaction. A payment up to $3,000 is 2.9 percent plus 30 cents. A payment between $3,001 and $10,000 is 2.5 percent plus 30 cents.

- **SQUARE:** This is a card swiper plugged into your iPhone, iPad or Android device. (No monthly fee, only a 2.75 percent per-swipe fee).

- **LAWPAY:** Specifically designed for lawyers, you can process multiple bank accounts, e.g., trust account or operating account. ($20 per month service fee, plus 20 cents per transaction and 1.95 percent per transaction).

- **YOUR BANK:** The bank where you maintain your firm's trust account and operating account can receive electronic payments.

✓ **Special considerations for fees that must be deposited in a trust account:**

- Trust account violations are one of the most common reasons for disciplinary actions.

- Confirm that your State's Rules of Professional Conduct permit you to accept credit card payments for your IOLTA or Client Trust Account, as some states prohibit it.

- Electronic payments are subject to transaction fees, chargebacks, and chargeback penalties.

- State rules and advisory opinions vary widely on how

to manage credit card transaction fees and chargeback fees. Follow your state rules, and keep in mind the two fundamental rules:

- ☐ No commingling of attorney and client funds.
- ☐ Client funds must be available upon request and without delay.

- While normally it is impermissible to commingle the lawyer's own funds with client funds, it is generally permissible when necessary to pay banking and transaction fees. Consult your state's rules for specific details.

✓ **Nonrefundable Fees**

- Nonrefundable retainers or flat fees violate public policy/ rules of professional conduct.

✓ **Discuss out-of-pocket costs**

- Court filing fees
- Proper service of process fees
- Private investigator fees
- Depositions and deposition transcripts
- Expert witness fees
- Mediation
- Trial exhibits
- Outsourced photocopies
- Medical records
- Jury fees
- Travel
- Postage
- Long-distance phone calls

✓ **Treat your invoices as marketing tools**

- Design attractive invoices that convey your firm's logo (doing so projects distinctive professionalism).

- Use the same design for marketing messages.
- What every law invoice should contain:
  - ☐ Your business name and address details.
  - ☐ The name and address of the company you are invoicing (and the contact name if you have one).
  - ☐ A unique invoice reference/number that will relate to this invoice only.
- A date for the invoice (which will generally be the date on which the invoice is created—or in accounting parlance, "raised").
- A list of the services that you have provided, line-by-line, and the cost of each of these.
- A total amount for the invoice.
- The payment terms for the invoice (i.e., how long the customer has to pay).
- Telephone/fax contact numbers.
- Company email address.
- Details on how to pay, including firm's account and routing numbers.

✓ **The secrets to billing**[24]

- Bill punctually and strategically:
  - ☐ Payment due upon receipt of invoice.
  - ☐ Bill when your perceived value is greatest. As each day passes after a successful outcome, the perception of your value is diminished.
- Send out invoice right after a positive outcome.
- Break down the value of every service you provide.
- Be detailed, be accurate.

---

24 http://www.americanbar.org/publications/gpsolo_ereport/2011/november_2011/billing_ethical-ly_getting_paid.html

- Remember that lawyer's bills are sometimes subject to discovery. Carefully redact work descriptions to avoid inadvertently tipping off the other side about strategy.

- If a client is going to receive settlement payments, be paid before the money is issued or dissipated.

- You cannot double-bill for paralegal time.

- Lawyers may not split fees with paralegals.

- Lawyers may offer a compensation plan to include paralegal bonuses based on productivity and firm profitability.

- Ask before exceeding budget—if one has been established.

- Estimate advance court costs and have an agreed-upon retainer deposited into the trust account to avoid footing upfront costs.

- Think long-term (a friendly bill makes a client maintain an ongoing relationship).

- Communicate before sending the invoice.

- Be candid about cost-effective strategies (short concise emails or text messages will save the client $, rather than long rambling phone conversations).

✓ **Be clear about consequences of non-payment**

- Fee agreement must include a clause that if you don't get paid pursuant to your fee agreement or "payment plan," you have a right to withdraw from the case.

- You must give reasonable notice that you intend to withdraw from the case unless payment is received.

- Note that any disputes between attorney and client should be referred in the first instance to non-binding mediation or arbitration.

- Specify the client's right to terminate the attorney.

- Detail attorney's obligations after termination or withdrawal:

☐ Attorney must take reasonable steps to protect client's interest.

☐ Deliver papers and property to which client is entitled, or take reasonable steps to do so.

☐ Refund any fees that have not been earned.

☐ Property that is not returned must be held in safekeeping for a period of time. The ABA model proscribes 5 years. But check your jurisdiction to find the required number of years.

✓ **Create a firm collection policy**

- Keep track of delinquent clients.

- Have staff call or send a letter, more than once.

- Be flexible, but don't back down—you deserve to be paid!

- Ask clients to inform you in advance if payment is delayed.

- Fee agreement: "The client agrees that should any invoice remain unpaid for (30-60-90 days), the attorney will cease working on the matter, and if the matter is in court, the client agrees to the attorney's withdrawal.

- Send out invoices on or about the 25th of the month.

✓ **Maintain goodwill when a matter is concluded**

- The end of the case shouldn't mean the end of the relationship.

- Your current clients are your absolute best referral sources.

- Always conduct an exit interview, and when you send a closing letter, consider it a marketing letter too.

✓ **Beware: Big Case, Big Fee**

- Do you have the experience?

- Do you have the staff support to handle it?

- If on contingency, can you afford to finance the case?

- Could you bring on another lawyer?

20
Getting Set Up: Law Practice Financial Management

Regardless of your fee structure, nowadays, using technology and state-of-the-art software, billing accurately should be a non-issue. Who could have believed a decade ago that we could track our time by using timekeeping apps on our phones or mobile devices?

Visit the Ironman resource page at www.PracticeLawLikeAnIronman.com/resources for more accounting suggestions and tips to help make your practice run more efficiently

Now, once you have your fee structure and billing system in place, it's time to consider a number of other financial matters:

- **HIRE A CPA**
  - Accounting and record-keeping
  - Tax advice
  - Auditing
  - Coordinate services with in-house bookkeeping applications.
  - Best way to find one: your attorney, banker, or business colleague, or the Society of Certified Public Accountants in your state.

- **MAINTAIN PROPER RECORDS**[25]
  - A sufficient audit trail requires proper documentation.
  - Keep all deposit slips:
    - ☐ Date of deposit
    - ☐ Amount of deposit
    - ☐ Trust identification
    - ☐ Bank stamp confirming deposit
  - Keep checkbook stub (or voucher, for voucher-type checks) that shows when and to whom the lawyer disbursed the funds.
  - Keep all bank receipts and statements.
  - Sign your own checks; even online payments print on copy paper for signature.
  - Review your Profit & Loss statement monthly to understand your expenses.
  - Review/reconcile all credit card statements.
  - Review/reconcile all loan payments with bank to be sure your amortization matches the bank's amortization.
  - With any new vendor, obtain a W-9 if going to 1099 at the end of the year.
  - Have a filing system, bills paid by vendor, box and label at the end of the year.
  - Keep copies of all checks issued to disburse funds.
  - Check or checks that the lawyer issued to disburse the trust funds should show:
    - ☐ The date the lawyer issued the check.
    - ☐ The amount for which the lawyer issued the check.

25 *Lawyers' Trust Accounts: A Handbook on The Rules Governing the Duties of Lawyers to Account for Client Funds and Property,* 2nd edition. John J. Mueller

- ☐ The name of the payee or person to whom the lawyer issued the check.

- ☐ The purpose for which the lawyer issued the check.

- ☐ The order in which the holders of the check negotiated or transferred it.

- ☐ The date the payee deposited or negotiated it.

- ☐ The date each party in the collection process negotiated or transferred the check.

- • If a client disappears or cannot be located:

  - ☐ The funds still belong to the client.

  - ☐ The lawyer must take reasonable steps to locate the client.

4

- ■ **HIRE AN OFFICE BOOKKEEPER, whose duties include the following:**[26]

  - Develops a system for all financial transactions, prescribing bookkeeping policies and procedures.

  - Maintains subsidiary accounts by verifying, allocating, and posting transactions.

  - Balances subsidiary accounts by reconciling entries.

  - Maintains general ledger by transferring subsidiary account summaries.

  - Balances general ledger by preparing a trial balance; reconciling entries.

  - Maintains historical records by filing documents.

  - Prepares financial reports by collecting, analyzing, and summarizing account information and trends.

26 https://hiring.monster.com/hr/hr-best-practices/recruiting-hiring-advice/job-descriptions/book-keeper-job-description-sample.aspx

- Complies with federal, state, and local legal requirements by studying requirements; enforcing adherence to requirements; filing reports; advising management on needed actions.

- Contributes to team effort by accomplishing related results as needed.

- Set up all payroll tax payments for electronic filing. Penalties for late payments are high.

- Use a payroll service if not comfortable with payroll process.

- Always have employees fill out and sign government withholding forms.

- Make sure to understand Workers Comp for the state you are in; all states have their own process for compensation insurance.

- Watch for odd payment schedules (phone bill paid 2x in a month).

- Watch for payroll amounts higher than expected – timesheet inflation.

- Watch for odd charges on your credit cards.

- **MAINTAIN METICULOUS RECORDS of business-related expenses and firm finances.**

  - Fixed monthly expenses:

    - ☐ Rent or mortgage payment
    - ☐ Utilities
    - ☐ Payroll
    - ☐ Taxes
    - ☐ Insurance
    - ☐ Equipment
    - ☐ Periodicals

☐ Membership fees for professional associations

      ☐ Lease on furniture

      ☐ Library and/or books

      ☐ Office supplies

      ☐ Promotional events

      ☐ Automobile costs

      ☐ Travel

      ☐ Entertaining

      ☐ Accountant

      ☐ Bank fees

      ☐ Loan payments

      ☐ Equipment maintenance

      ☐ Software updates

      ☐ Marketing/advertising expenses

- Variable expenses
- Long-term projections of fees, expenses, cash for 3-5 years

4

- **Are you keeping ACCURATE AND TIMELY RECORDs of:**
  - Accounts receivable?
  - Accounts payable?
  - Payroll?
  - Your trust account or IOLTA[27] account?

- **HAVE YOU ORDERED CHECKS?**
  - Checking
  - IOLTA
  - Savings

---

27 http://www.mtjustice.org/wp-content/uploads/2017/03/WHAT-IS-IOLTA-6_23_16-2.pdf

- Do you have a **LAW PRACTICE CREDIT CARD?**

- Do you keep your **EXPENSE RECEIPTS ORGANIZED** by month?

- Can you **PROVIDE A LIST** of everything you offer the client so that you can show what they are paying for?

- Have you decided your billing methods?

- Contingent fees, hourly billing, or fixed-price?

- Do you have a system for collecting fees?

- Do you have a fee agreement?

- Does your fee agreement communicate specifically how the client will be billed or charged?

- How did you determine that your rates are competitive?

- Do you have spreadsheets that cover different financial aspects of your practice?

- Spreadsheets that contain information on income, expenses, when bills are due, information on due dates of owed money?

- A time billing program?

- Do you have your deposit slips?

- Do you have order slips for when you need to order new checks or deposit slips?

21
Tips on Handling Client Funds and Property

When you receive funds or property belonging to a client, you hold those funds or property in **TRUST.**

- **Two kinds of trust accounts**
  - **CLIENT TRUST ACCOUNT (CTA)**
    - ☐ Interest bearing account opened on behalf of a single client.
    - ☐ Earned interest benefits the client.
    - ☐ Appropriate for an amount large enough and held long enough that the interest earned will exceed the fees associated with the account.
  - **IOLTA**
    - ☐ Interest-on-lawyer's trust account opened to hold client funds.
    - ☐ Appropriate when the potential interest will not exceed the costs associated with managing a unique client trust account.
    - ☐ Required in most jurisdictions.
    - ☐ Interest is remitted to the state for charitable purposes such as legal aid for indigent clients.
- **In determining whether to establish a CTA rather than deposit funds into your IOLTA, consider:**
  - The amount of the funds

- Expected duration of the deposit
- Interest rate to be earned on the deposit
- The cost of establishing and administering the CTA including service charges, cost of lawyer services, and cost of preparing any tax reports.
- Any other circumstances that affect the ability of the client's funds to earn a net return for the client.

- **An account record must show the following:**
  - What the lawyer received
  - When the lawyer received it
  - What the lawyer did with it
  - When the lawyer did what he/she did

- **Your fiduciary duties are the following,** as defined by John J. Mueller in his book, *Lawyer's Trust Accounts: A Handbook On the Rules Governing the Duties of Lawyers To Account for Client Funds and Property:*
  - To safeguard the client assets
  - To record when you accepted the funds
  - To place them in a separate interest-bearing account in a financial institution authorized to do business in your state.
  - To segregate them from your personal and business assets.
  - To account to the owner of the funds (or property).
  - To make immediately available funds to client.
  - To deposit securities, negotiable instruments, jewelry, and other like valuables in a safe or a safe deposit box.
  - To keep records of such property after the termination of the representation or the appropriate disbursement of property for the period of years designated in your jurisdiction.

- To deposit funds in an IOLTA only when the funds represent a minimal amount or if the lawyer will hold the funds only for a brief period of time.

- To render a full accounting of funds and property.

- To provide the client or owner of the property with the lawyer's detailed, written records concerning the funds or property.

■ **Steps to take if you make a mistake concerning a client trust**

- If you disburse too little money to a client, send a check for the balance of funds owed.

- If you disburse too much money, arrange a refund.

- If client declines to refund, commence a civil action to recover the excess from the client. Also, review your professional liability policy to see whether you have coverage for civil claims arising because of this error.

- Take steps to assure you have the resources to cover any shortfall in the trust funds.

- Refrain from depositing your funds in the trust account to cover any shortfall, and consult with a professional responsibility lawyer.

- If you discover that you or another staff member has inadvertently deposited money intended for the trust account into the operating account or non-trust account, immediately move the funds to the proper account.

- If you discover that you or another staff member has inadvertently deposited money intended for the operating account into the trust account, immediately transfer the funds to the proper account.

- If you discover unauthorized charges to or withdrawals from a trust account, immediately notify the bank.

- • If you discover a forgery or unauthorized signature or material alteration of the trust by one of your staff and you carry fidelity insurance, immediately submit a claim.

- ■ **Delegation of duties**
  - • The lawyer bears liability for any breach of the fiduciary duties, even breaches resulting from ignorance, negligent omission, or negligent commission.
  - • The lawyer remains liable if a delegated person improperly performs the duties.
  - • Courts condemn mishandling of entrusted funds even when the mishandling results from nothing more sinister than poor management.

Note: As the American Bar Association states in Rule 1.15: Safekeeping Property:

"A lawyer may deposit his own funds into the client trust account for the sole purpose of paying or obtaining a waiver of bank service charges on that account, but only in an amount necessary for that purpose."

Also, an attorney must promptly distribute all portions of the funds or other property on which the interests are not in dispute. In other words, when an attorney earns his fee, he or she may distribute it to his own personal account.

- ■ **If it's undisputed that the lawyer has earned the fee, then the lawyer must promptly distribute fees from funds held in trust when there is no dispute concerning the amount of the fee.**

NOTE: *Comingling occurs even though the lawyer has kept a sufficient balance in his personal account to repay the comingled funds and the lawyer could have returned the client funds at any time on demand.*

PART FIVE

THE RIGHT STUFF

22
Teambuilding and Firm Leadership

"A rising tide lifts all boats."
– John F. Kennedy, (1917-1963) –

In order to marshal forces and organize the staffing logistics of a solo practice, you must be a great *leader*, **someone who can translate vision into reality with:**

- ✓ **Indisputable expertise**
- ✓ **High standards**
- ✓ **Self-discipline**
- ✓ **Communications skills**
- ✓ **Peak physical energy**
- ✓ **A positive vision of the future**
- ✓ **Organized plans to get there**
- ✓ **Role-model skills to:**
    - Set an example
    - Delegate
    - Inspire
    - Challenge the status quo

As **THEODORE ROOSEVELT** once said:

"The best executive is the one who has sense enough to pick good men to do what he wants done, and self-restraint enough to keep from meddling with them while they do it."

To do this requires the ability to hire a great team, plus active preparation... mastering the nuts-and-bolts of office set-up, reading motivational books, listening to audiobooks and podcasts, attending seminars and conferences, and participating in continuing education too. It's like training for that triathlon.

You need to:

- ✓ Sharpen your focus
- ✓ Hone your physical stamina
- ✓ Practice positive affirmations to foster confidence and emotional strength

5

But even with a vision, determination, and preparation, being a great leader doesn't necessarily translate as being a great manager. The two are not synonymous.

Leaders have people who *follow* them, while managers have people who *work* for them. It's your job to convey to your manager your picture of the business as you envision it.

<u>LEADERSHIP</u> qualities include: [28]

- **Passion**
- **Decisiveness**
- **Vision**
- **Boldness**
- **Imagination**
- **Persistence**
  - Definiteness of purpose
  - Burning desire
  - Self-reliance
  - Accurate knowledge
  - Willpower
  - Ingrained habits for positivity
- **Courage**
- **Focus**
- **Confidence**
- **Charisma**
- **Curiosity**
- **Commitment**
- **Responsibility**
- **Open-mindedness**
- **Authenticity**
- **Integrity**
- **Positivity**
- **Inspiration**

---

28 https://www.entrepreneur.com/article/270486

- Resiliency
- Assertiveness
- Adaptability
- Conscientiousness

MANAGEMENT qualities:[29]

- An optimistic attitude
- Accountability
- Honesty
- Emotional maturity
- Patience
- Flexibility
- Prioritization
- Warmth and competence
- Being detail-oriented
- Being highly organized
- Operating with a short-range view
- Being mindful of the bottom line
- Loyalty to the leader
- Effective decision-making
- Willingness to develop talent

5

As *Business Insider* summarizes: [30]

- A manager tells; a leader sells.
- A manager plans the details; a leader sets the direction.
- A manager minimizes risks; a leader takes them.

29 http://www.phdinmanagement.org/25-qualities-and-characteristics-of-a-good-manager.html
30 http://www.businessinsider.com/biggest-differences-between-managers-and-leaders-2016-3

- A manager instructs employees; a leader encourages people.
- A manager has objectives; a leader has vision.
- A manager meets expectations; a leader charts new growth.
- A manager eyes the bottom line; the leader eyes the horizon.
- A manager sees a problem; a leader sees an opportunity.
- A manager thinks short-term; a leader thinks long-term.
- A manager follows the map; a leader carves new roads.
- A manager approves; a leader motivates.
- A manager establishes rules; a leader breaks them.
- A manager assigns duties; a leader fosters ideas.
- A manager relies on control; a leader inspires trust.

In short, as you evolve as a leader, you'll see that your workday is comprised of:

- ✓ Decisions to be made
- ✓ Problems to be tackled

5

Use this checklist to organize your Office protocol: [31]

- ✓ Define what you want to accomplish and why.
- ✓ Collect the facts from multiple resources.
- ✓ Ask the right questions (do more listening than talking).
- ✓ Take no one into your confidence except members of your "mastermind" group and/or mentor.

---

31 *Think And Grow Rich*, Napoleon Hill

✓ Know what is motivating your decision.

✓ Consider 2-3 possible working solutions, prioritizing the best.

✓ Keep your options open but don't procrastinate.

✓ Trust your intuition.

✓ Keep perspective, reflecting on the results you're seeing.

✓ Pull the switch!—and make the decision (i.e., solve the problem).

✓ Trust in your ability to expand your viewpoint and remain flexible.

AND REMEMBER:

- The staff members that helped you make any decision must be thanked and appreciated.

- The colleagues that provided advice or insight into case law must also be thanked.

  - A lawyer who takes time to help you is taking away time he could be using to do something that's billable.

  - Don't just say "thanks." Hand write a personal thank-you note, send a thoughtful gift, invite that person out to lunch or to happy hour. **In other words, don't be a taker. Instead, be a great people person.**

23
People Skills and the Art of Listening

To improve your people skills, consider a few of the themes referenced in **John C. Maxwell's *Winning with People* and in Dale Carnegie's *How to Win Friends and Influence People*:**

- Are you a positive or a negative person?
- Do you spend time with positive people or negative people?
- Are you comfortable with yourself? (if not, you cannot be comfortable with others).
- Do you have a plan to improve your attitude?
- Can you lift people up and add value to their lives?
- Can you commit to encouraging others and do it daily?
- Do you talk about your own mistakes before criticizing others?
- When critiquing an employee, do you allow them to save face?
- Can you try to see things from another person's perspective?
- Do you listen and encourage others to talk about themselves?
- Do you make others feel appreciated?
- Do you avoid arguing with someone who is cold, arrogant, or stubborn?
- Can you try to make the confrontation into a win-win situation for both parties without becoming angry or accusatory?
- Are you calm and in control of your temper?

- When dealing with a gossiper at work, how do you redirect them?
- As the boss, are you approachable?
- Do you have a captivating smile?
- Does your tone of voice radiate interest and enthusiasm?
- Do you have a system for remembering names?
- Is your mood consistent?
- Do you have the ability to forgive easily and ask for forgiveness?
- Are you patient with others?
- Do you encourage your staff to celebrate their successes?
- well-being?

Above all, in the preliminary process of building your solo practice, you must also **TRAIN YOURSELF TO BE A GREAT LISTENER,** whether talking to staff, clients, or members of the court. **Here are some great tips from *The Customer Rules: The 39 Essential Rules for Delivering Sensational Service* by Lee Cockerell:**

5

- Talk less—and focus more on the other person.
- Always make eye contact.
- Avoid interrupting.
- Reflect, summarize, and paraphrase what you're hearing.
- Use verbal affirmations, phrases that support what you're hearing.
- Ask open-ended questions (that the person will enjoy answering).
- Be aware of your mental and physical responses.
- Nod and smile at the speaker as appropriate.

- Make them feel valued.
- End the conversation by asking if there is anything else to discuss.

As you delve more into the art of focusing on what people are saying to you, be aware that there are **FIVE MAIN FORMS OF LISTENING,** as explained in John Jantsch's book *Duct Tape Marketing:*

- **PASSIVE LISTENING:** You're hearing the words, but sitting quietly without responding to what the speaker is saying, really just waiting for your turn to speak. You might offer a few open-ended replies, but this kind of listening requires minimal verbal feedback from the listener (more commonly used by husbands and wives than lawyers and clients, for sure!).

- **ACTIVE LISTENING:** Often used in counseling, training, and conflict resolution, this type of listening requires an active interplay between both speaker and listener (certainly used in court proceedings, arbitrations, depositions, and in all client/attorney interactions).

- **REFLECTIVE LISTENING:** This involves two steps... seeking to understand a speaker's idea, then paraphrasing the idea back to the speaker to confirm it has been understood (a strong tool in your arsenal for all human relationships, professional or otherwise).

- **SELECTIVE LISTENING:** I'd compare this to a student with a highlighter. You focus on high priority information and skim over the rest. This allows space for multitasking and planning what you're going to say next, an opening to pitch yourself (not to be used with clients who require 100 percent of your attention).

- **PERCEPTIVE LISTENING:** This is the most complex form
  of listening, as it requires you to be totally focused on what
  you're hearing, while also considering what the person
  isn't saying—the subtext of what they might be thinking
  (therapists use this kind of listening, though any great
  salesman will use it as well).

You can effectively use these distinct listening skills
in all your relationships, including with staff members,
clients, colleagues, and court officials.

As an aside, **to more finely attune your listening skills, you can also
practice just *listening in space,*** a form of meditation that sensitizes
you to lending an ear, as summarized in John Jantsch's book *The
Commitment Engine: Making Work Worth It*

- Find a quiet place and close your eyes.
- Now empty your thoughts and begin carefully listening
  to the sounds immediately noticeable in close proximity
  (the sounds from the street, the hum of the heater or air-
  conditioner, the presence of someone nearby).
- Now direct your listening farther, focus on the street sounds
  of cars passing by or construction work.
- Then direct your ear just as far as you can—maybe to an
  airplane or train sounds, the rumble of a subway.

5

By doing this, you're refining your ability to listen to and
understand what's going on all around you, just like vision
impaired people who depend on their ears to guide them.

24
Hire the Attitude, Teach the Skills

Armed as you may be with great skills, *a leader* **is only as good as the staff;** the people who are your prime support and safety network. It's this team that allows you the freedom to practice law and comfortably delegate a multitude of tasks. To lead effectively, you must create a crack team of people, a strong inner circle of paid staff, enhanced by supportive colleagues, friends, and family.

MOTHER TERESA put it best:

"You can do what I cannot do. I can do what you cannot do. Together we can do great things."

So from the start, you will:

- **Hire** a staff that has great team chemistry and cohesiveness.
- **Nurture,** protect, and guide them.
- **Support** interaction with staff as your work family .
- **Instill** an office atmosphere of trust and good will.
- **Earn** role-model status, as a reputable practitioner of high standards.
- **Prove** that employee efforts are directly contributive to your own success.
- **Celebrate** their victories.
- **Guide** them to recognize their strengths and weaknesses.
- **Encourage** "hard conversations" amongst them to foster growth.

In short, as the leader, you must demonstrate "emotional intelligence," which involves:

✓ Identifying your emotions and those of others

✓ **The maturity to control your emotions and not allow them to determine your actions** (e.g. the ability to calm down when you're upset).

✓ **Balancing work and play**

✓ **Embracing change**

✓ **Empathy**

✓ **Knowing your strengths and weaknesses**

✓ **Being self-motivated**

✓ **Not dwelling in the past**

✓ **Focusing on the positive**

✓ **Setting boundaries** (knowing how to say no, or redirect, yet being polite and compassionate).

The ultimate result of exercising emotional intelligence is an enhancement of **harmony** and **productivity, which is key to running any office efficiently. Simply put,**

People must get along. They need to be able to express themselves… and have fun.

In order to boost productivity, you should constructively create an atmosphere of friendly **competition; a dynamic that keeps everyone on their toes, ready to perform at the top of their game.** It's like an athletic competition, in which each member of the team pushes the others forward. Someone great next to you always makes you even better.

177

As **NAPOLEON HILL** wrote,

"When two or more people coordinate in a spirit of harmony and work toward a definite objective, they place themselves in a position, through that alliance, to absorb power directly from the great universal storehouse of infinite intelligence."

In less fancy words, the office works much better!

* * * * *

In the end, you're the leader and can decide on the level of authority to be delegated to your manager, someone empowered to oversee your firm.

The choice you make on this hire is critical.

A great office administrator and/or legal secretary is your **"general,"** someone who will maximize efficiency, nurture skills, and develop talent. You may not be able to afford such a person at the start, but once you can, the salary paid will pay itself back in spades.

This is someone you will trust implicitly, someone who can:

✓ Execute and improve your firm's day-to-day operations

✓ Understand your mission and vision statements

✓ Communicate effectively with lawyers, staff, and clients

✓ Make a commitment

✓ Make principle-based decisions

✓ Create momentum

178

- ✓ Be responsible
- ✓ Epitomize steadiness when problems arise
- ✓ Be disciplined

In terms of specific skill sets, your legal secretary and/or office manager must:

- Answer the phone and systematize message-taking
- Oversee time scheduling,
- Manage incoming and outgoing emails
- Supervise legal correspondence with clients and courts
- Manage personnel:
    - Screen new applicants
    - Mentor, coach, and train hired employees, providing constructive, respectful feedback.
    - Set performance examples and quality control
    - Perform annual evaluations
    - Allocate and prioritize workload assignments
    - Hire and fire (with input, final decision by you).
- Order supplies
- Update, close, and archive client files
- Manage technology maintenance (computers, phone systems, software).
- Monitor office expenses, guarding against inefficiency and waste.
- Oversee record-keeping and bills (payment of all operating costs, tracking. incoming and outgoing funds).
- Run credit cards and take payments from clients
- Make bank deposits

5

- **Issue checks** (the lawyer/owner must sign the checks)
- **Interact with vendors and office maintenance**
- **Handle customer complaints and requests**
- **Interface with marketing and public relations consultants**

Whew! That may sound like a description of Superman (or Woman), but you can and will find a motivated (and kind-hearted) person who can do all this and more. **As referenced in a *Best Legal Assistant blog of 2013*, what you're looking for is someone who must be or have:**

- **Proofreading and editing skills**
- **An ability to multi-task and establish priorities**
- **Highly organized for maintaining documents**
- **Research-oriented, adept in referencing relevant cases and laws associated with your case.**
- **Problem solver, proficient in finding solutions in what can be a highly-pressured environment.**
- **Professional and ethical**
- **A skilled communicator**
- **A good delegator**
- **Outstanding in word-processing and typing skills (this is optional, as digital technology makes high-speed typing less important).**
- **Adept with a digital dictating recorder and transcription unit (Olympus and Dragon).**

So who is going to become your office manager?

At first, that person may be you! Of course, you may also outsource part-time tasks to specialists, such as a law clerk to help out with practice governance issues, a secretary to manage court documents, a computer expert to fine-tune your systems, or a public relations and marketing consultant to establish your public profile.

But as your practice expands, you'll be able to afford a full-time legal secretary and/or experienced administrator with proven management skills.

ABOVE ALL: *Your office manager must be a team player.*

Sure, you could hire the most efficient and organized person in the world, but if their attitude is negative, and if they can't get along with others, your law firm will suffer. Nobody wants to deal with someone who is brusque, short-tempered, or has a know-it-all attitude.

Instead, they must exhibit:

- Friendliness
- Perseverance
- Patience
- Flexibility
- Eagerness to learn
- Desire to take on responsibility
- Positivity

Qualities like these are just as important as a candidate's résumé, because **your legal secretary/manager is your welcome mat to clients; the person they will interact with most.** So even if their résumé exhibits limited expertise in certain areas, it still might be a match.

MY MOTTO IS: *Hire the attitude—teach the skills.*

Why? It's because technical skills can be learned, whereas personalities aren't easily changed.

25
The Art of the Interview

Consider these points in your candidate search-and-interview process:

✓ Define <u>WHAT</u> you need and <u>WHO</u> you're looking for.

✓ Where will you place your ad?

✓ How will you screen applicants?

✓ What <u>RÉSUMÉ</u> criteria are essential and non-negotiable?

✓ Consider a group interview

- Create a verbal presentation for outlining the job.
- Ask applicants open-ended questions.
- Check their track records.
- Ask hard questions such as "Why did you leave the last job?"
- Assess how candidates interact with one another.
- Assess how they interact with your team.
- Meet with your team afterward to discuss choosing finalists.

✓ What tests should be administered?

✓ How will you check references?

✓ How many times will you interview finalists

✓ How will you conduct background checks?

✓ Once the hire is made, what is your probationary period?

✓ **Confer periodically with the new hire for 3 weeks and ask:**

- Were you fully aware of what was expected of you today?

- Were you able to do it?

- What problems or challenges did you face?

- What resources are required to enhance your job performance? After the probationary period ends, make a permanent decision.

✓ **Engage your staff in the recruiting process to increase the chance of a good fit, allowing the new hire to blend in.**

For additional ideas about interviewing protocol, visit: www.hireauthority.com.

As you will see, the interview process (and your communication with referral sources) **must assess:**

- **PERSONALITY:** Use the DISC personality test (www.123test.com/disc-personality-test/), a free diagnostic tool that pinpoints such personality types as driving, influencing, supporting, or calculating.

- **PASSION:** What motivates this person?
  - Workplace results?
  - Relationships?
  - Money?
  - Recognition?
  - Contribution?
  - Security?

- **PATTERN:** Look for a pattern of success (or failure) in the candidate's background, and assess whether they work best alone or on a team.

- **POTENTIAL:** Given the right mentoring, what might they accomplish for your practice?

5

- **PROFILE:** Gauge how well they blend into your established office culture and what chemistry they could have on your practice.

- **PLACEMENT:** Assess how they fit within your firm and what benefit they provide to your existing team.

In the end, within these broad categories, you're assessing candidate qualities like the ones listed below, **as summarized in *Mavericks at Work: Why the Most Original Minds in Business Win*, by William C. Taylor and Polly G. LaBarre:**

- Do they seem to be **upbeat** in nature?
- Are they **enthusiastic**?
- Are they **confident** but not egotistical?
- Are they **diplomatic** in handling clients?
- Are they **self-disciplined** and **organized**?
- Are they good **listeners**?
- Can they be a **pleasant persuader**?
- Are they **flexible** in their outlook?
- Are they **persistent problem solvers**?
- Will they be **accountable and committed**?
- Will they focus on people's **strengths**?
- Do they project a "**can-do**" **vibe**?
- Are they **goal-oriented** rather than limited in their self-belief?
- Can they work effectively as part of a **team**?
- Do they demonstrate **leadership** and **mentorship** skills?
- Will they **complement your weaknesses** and **encourage your strengths**?
- Can they **attract other leaders**?
- Will they be **loyal**?

5

- Are they ambitious, yet humble?
- Do they have a **warrior spirit**, someone with great vigor and courage
- Do they have a **genuine interest in other people?**

Conversely, here are a few things to keep in mind about employees with the **wrong** attitude:

- Are they unable to acknowledge mistakes?
- Are they unable to forgive?
- Do they harbor a grudge?
- Do they focus on petty jealousies?
- Are they intrinsically selfish?
- Are they judgmental and harsh?
- Do they want to claim all the credit?

Make sure that you do **not** hire those you sense have these qualities, and terminate any employee who develops a pattern of such attitudes. After all, if you care about your team, you need to separate the bad apples, so to speak, from the tree.

5

You must terminate employees who:
- ✓ Blame others for errors
- ✓ Raise false concerns about or criticize the work of others
- ✓ Make unreasonable demands
- ✓ Yell and scream threats of job loss, insults, or putdowns
- ✓ Demonstrate arbitrary enforcement of rules
- ✓ Exclude others from social engagement
- ✓ Steal credit for another's work

REMEMBER: *We bring all of who we are into our work and work relationships. This includes our hearts and souls, so who you hire is critical.*

I used to interview and hire job candidates solely on my own, with mixed results. I needed to incorporate into my process feedback from my trusted inner circle of established employees. I value their reactions and opinions, especially since every office is a team effort, requiring a new candidate to blend in.

Rather dramatically, the first time we all weighed in on an applicant was when the poor woman became acutely sick at the interview. There she was, suffering from the flu, trying to smile and be pleasant, excusing herself twice to go to the bathroom. Yet, she answered all our questions extremely well and we wound up hiring her. Why?

- She wanted the internship so much that she didn't call in sick
- She demonstrated fortitude, ambition and guts
- • She handled herself with poise and confidence

Our decision to hire her turned out to be a great one, and to this day, we're a team of five with great team chemistry.

My firm's legal paralegal, Jennifer Blum, made up a list of her own criteria for hiring staff. As she always says, **first and foremost is a candidate's <u>attitude</u> and <u>work-ethic:</u>**

"We want to hire people who have had an inherent entrepreneurial streak. Growing up, were they paper boys or babysitters, caddies or lawn-mowers? Did they shovel snow or sell Girl Scout cookies?"

186

Jen looks for:

- ✓ Solid background with a demonstrable work ethic
- ✓ Go-getter personality, someone who makes things happen.
- ✓ Integrity, honesty and does what they say they will do.
- ✓ Great smile and attitude
- ✓ High energy level
- ✓ Personal warmth
- ✓ Courteous, personable phone manner
- ✓ Tolerance
- ✓ Sense of HUMOR
- ✓ Spirit of service and cooperation
- ✓ Discretion and self-control
- ✓ Professional appearance and good self-image
- ✓ Trainable, open and flexible in thinking.
- ✓ Adaptable

With a combination of traits like these, you will have the time you need for meeting with established or prospective clients, writing briefs, going to court, arguing motions, and preparing for trials or hearings.

26

Hiring a Paralegal

A paralegal can be a powerful enhancement to any solo law practice, taking on the work that lawyers are overqualified to do.

By hiring a paralegal, you transfer billable work to them while gradually increasing your own side of the practice, thus boosting firm profits. (If you can't afford a full-time paralegal, there are many contractors who will work part-time.)

REMEMBER: *A paralegal is not there as a typist, filing clerk, or someone to run errands. And a paralegal cannot do the following:*

- ✓ **Accept a case or set a fee**
- ✓ **Give legal advice**
- ✓ **Plan legal strategy**
- ✓ **Take a deposition or handle a hearing or trial**

But a highly skilled paralegal is your legal right hand, freeing you to do more sophisticated work at a higher hourly rate.

You have a paralegal because you obviously can't do all the work yourself, **so you must learn how to effectively delegate:**

- ✓ Delegate assignments in writing with instructions, deadline dates, references, and resources
- ✓ Set up reporting requirements, e.g., via email, memo, telephone, or in-person
- ✓ Allow time for the paralegal to discuss prioritized and workload issues with you
- ✓ Provide feedback, constructive criticism, evaluation
- ✓ Guard against work overload
- ✓ Prepare a procedural form for each task/ assignment, including:
  - Name of client and case number if used
  - Billing information
  - Assignment being delegated
  - Deadline for completion
  - An estimate of the amount of time required for the task
  - References to resources or persons needed
  - Copies to other persons working on the client matter
  - A special notation that the assignment is urgent

5

So where do you recruit a paralegal?

- ■ **PARALEGAL EDUCATION PROGRAMS**
  - Check the ABA website for approved programs
  - Acquire references for qualified candidates
- ■ **PARALEGAL ASSOCIATIONS**
  - National Association of Legal Assistants (NALA)
  - National Federation of Paralegal Association (NFPA)
- ■ **ADVERTISEMENTS in general-interest and legal newspapers, Legal Associations Journals**

- **PLACEMENT WEBSITES** (monster.com, Ziprecruiter.com, or Indeed.com)
- **PROFESSIONAL EMPLOYMENT AGENCIES**
- **INTERNSHIP PROGRAMS** (www.internships.com)

The evaluation of paralegal applicants should cover the following:

- ✓ YOUR expectations
- ✓ THEIR knowledge and skills
- ✓ THEIR ability to become part of a team

Consider giving extensive in-house training to your paralegals on the following topics:

- Lexis and Westlaw training
- Ethics
- E-Discovery
- Preparing answers and complaints
- Responding to discovery requests
- Preparing and serving subpoenas
- File organization
- Organizing records for expert and attorney review
- Preparing the attorney for witness interviews, depositions, and court conferences.
- Preparing motions
- Drafting settlement statements
- Preparing for and assisting at trial and motion hearings
- Preparing public records requests
- Interviewing and taking statements of witnesses
- Internet research

27

Mission-Critical Tasks Come First: DELEGATION

In the end, whether it's hiring a paralegal, a legal secretary, and/or an office manager, I can tell you that putting a great staff together is like casting a play. You get the right people for the right parts and then you go into rehearsals, refining the production.

So once your entire team is established, the efficiency of your office is an equation:

DELEGATION + PRIORITIZATION + ACCOUNTABILITY = PRODUCTIVITY

Your employees must:

- ✓ Meet deadlines
- ✓ Divide their time wisely
- ✓ Distinguish between high and low-priority tasks

To succeed as a leader, you must:

- ✓ <u>PRIORITIZE ALL WORK ASSIGNMENTS</u> (in order of importance, from urgent to mundane).
- ✓ <u>MAP OUT</u> in-office conferences and out-of-office client meetings and court dates.

✓ **USE DRIVE TIME WISELY** (return phone calls, confer with staff, listen to audiobooks and podcasts).

✓ **PLACE TOP-LEVEL PRIORITIES** into your electronic calendar with alerts.

✓ **ESTIMATE** the amount of time needed to complete each task (leave wiggle room).

✓ **SET A MEETING PROTOCOL.**

- At a minimum, meet weekly for one hour. Then reduce staff meetings to once a month, when all systems are operating efficiently.

- Solicit staff suggestions for changes or improvements.

- Prepare a written agenda and distribute in advance of meeting.

- Include supporting documents.

- Confirm staff understanding of purpose of the meeting.

- Ask invitees to confirm their attendance.

- Send out a reminder the day before the meeting.

- Advise participants of their roles at the meeting.

- Emphasize the importance of being ON TIME.

- Reserve a specific time and keep to it (no open-ended meetings).

- Assign a timekeeper.

- Have a staff member take minutes; type, and later distribute.

- Establish a format that allows an organized sequence of questions and answers, allowing all to express their opinions without judgment or ridicule. When disagreement arises, look for points of agreement for the overall goal to be achieved.

5

- Free-flowing discussion
- Time limits for sharing
- Who will participate in the meeting

✓ **CONCLUDE THE MEETING with a summary of decisions made, an action plan, and the next steps needed to accomplish your purpose.**

- Set deadlines for follow-through and accountability.
- Provide positive reinforcement using thanks and praise of staff members.
- All these factors should be memorialized in a meeting template, to be used repeatedly (for further information on meeting structure and development, see: www.meetingresult.com).

✓ **EXERCISE DELEGATION** — the outsourcing of projects to staff and vendors—from office equipment and computer software issues to hiring and firing (hopefully more hiring than firing once you learn to hire correctly). I delegate in order to maximize my time for what I do best: practicing law, going to court, meeting with clients, and marketing my practice. **Figure out the things you won't do, or can't do well, and assign the job to others, using the following criteria:**

- Is doing it myself the best use of my time?
- Is it my strength?
- Do I have the requisite expertise to complete the task effectively?
- Do I enjoy it?
- Is it at the core of what I get paid for?
- Does it require my skills or personal touch?
- Is it something I can teach staff members to do?

5

- Will it make my staff more independent, more invested in our work?

- Can I outsource it? If something you are doing can be done 80 percent as well by someone else, delegate it!

- Can technology aid in getting it done more quickly than I could?

- Will it cost less (for me or the client) if someone else does it?

✓ **Realize that you can't do everything yourself, which will result in:**

- A backlog of work

- Clients becoming dissatisfied

- Underuse of the staff

- Jeopardy of the financial growth of the firm

REMEMBER: *Growth requires delegation, NOT abdication.*

5

So always use these steps for effective delegation:

✓ **Give clear and comprehensive instructions** about the scope of the project with designated maximum time limits and "check-in" times.

✓ **Ensure that you have been understood** by encouraging questions, fostering a relaxed atmosphere.

✓ **Set realistic deadlines** and build in time for the unexpected.

✓ **Establish benchmarks** and check-ins to ensure that your staff members are on-track before they complete the task.

✓ **Evaluate and share the outcome,** giving both praise and critical feedback, a key part of disciplined delegation. Otherwise, you can't expect staff to grow and improve. Remember, positive feedback motivates employees to improve and fosters loyalty. Always review the work product and process with your staff, to streamline and improve the process.

✓ **Differentiate strategic work that you must do** (includes practicing law in and out of court, plus having a global view of all the tasks required in your practice), from tactical work that others can do, (such as filing, billing, answering the phone, transcriptions, going to the bank).

✓ **Tactical work includes:**

- Opening mail
- Stuffing outgoing envelopes
- Filing copies of documents
- Running errands
- Doing court and administrative filings
- Photocopying
- Going to the post office
- Answering phones
- Word processing
- Returning telephone calls when you cannot
- Downloading and printing out email
- Maintaining your calendar and tickler system
- Proofreading
- Discovery
- Drafting

- Marking exhibits and exhibit preparation
- Litigation preparation

✓ **Keep a handy list** of "things to do" between meetings or waiting in court:

- Return phone calls
- Answer emails
- Write thank-you notes
- Read journals
- Review your things-to-do list

* * * * *

As your staff structure becomes established, ask yourself:

- Does your inner circle share your values, vision, and philosophy?
- Is your team open with you?
- Do you tell the truth to them, even when it hurts?
- Do they offer strengths in areas of your weaknesses?
- Do they have the power to influence others?
- Are you comfortable with them speaking on your behalf?
- Do they lift others up?
- Do they function well as a team and make one another better?
- Is there a sense of friendly competition among the staff?
- Do you give them credit when things go well?
- Do you hold them accountable when things fail?
- Do you avoid office politics and favoritism?

5

Now you need to provide staff with:

✓ **Training** (they need to know exactly what is expected at work).

  • Daily routines and processes

  • Client services

  • Document protocol

  • Knowledge of marketing and brand attributes

✓ **The equipment and technology to do the job.**

✓ **Praise and feedback for a job well done.**

✓ **Clear goals and realistic deadlines.**

✓ **A sense of autonomy** (think like an owner, not a clerk).

✓ **An understanding of the firm's finances.**

✓ **A safe and friendly workplace.**

✓ **Constructive feedback.**

✓ **Frequent and honest communication**

  • Is your staff a group of YES people, or directly honest?

  • Do you hold brainstorming sessions?

  • Do you hold team-building sessions?

  • Do you give employees a sense of ownership?

  • Do you praise their efforts?

  • Are disagreements respectful?

  • If a grudge develops, can you clear the air?

  • As a leader, are you a good listener?

  • Do you have an open-door policy?

✓ **Performance reviews**

  • Recognize employee accomplishments

  • Address any sub-par performance with constructive criticism

5

✓ **Continuing education**

- Attend CLE/Center for Professional Development/American Bar Association seminars, webinars, webcasts, teleconferences.
- Stock your office with books, videos, online courses (available to all employees).
- Reading
- Books on your area of practice
- Statutes updates
- Marketing manuals
- Self-motivational books

✓ **Join the American Bar Association's Law Practice Management Division**

Your job is to establish lasting commitments from employees. To accomplish this, you must:

5

✓ Make them feel they're part of the family.

✓ Celebrate their strengths.

✓ Make them winners.

✓ Let them stand out.

✓ Treat them as adults.

✓ Expose them to great events and to new people and places.

By engaging with your employees in these ways, you give them power to reach their own potential and to succeed for you.

28
The Power of Camaraderie
Don't Forget the Fun

When coping with the daily stresses of running a defense law practice, which includes guiding clients through intimidating court appearances, the ability to lighten things up at the office and laugh is key.

Sure, the practice of law is essentially a serious one, but there is always room for some levity with staff and clients. After all, people give their last dollar to be entertained, which is why I foster a relaxed office atmosphere, a firm that's both fun to hear from and fun to do business with.

Both employees and your clients benefit from a practice where play and laughter are as treasured as profit and process.

So don't be boring and dry from one end of the day to the other.

Think about Your Practice,

- **Do you make your employees or clients smile?**
- **Do you give them a delightful little surprise?**
- **Do you add play to the workplace?**
  - Send goofy gifts to customers
  - Answer the phone in a warm-hearted way
  - Create personal stories
  - Post pictures of your staff during the day

In our offices, here is our Top Ten Laughter List:

1. My distinctive unconventional use of the F*** word, usually directed at inanimate objects — a file cabinet falling on my foot, a briefcase emptying by mistake in the middle of the hallway, etc.

2. An overtired lawyer (me) falling asleep at his desk, documented in cell phone pictures taken by staff (who know not to wake me up unless there is an emergency).

3. Team retreats — getaways to bond, have fun, and focus on agenda issues.

4. St. Patrick's Day extravaganza, i.e., Steve wearing a green pinstriped suit, taking the staff out to a string of Irish bars, lots of bonding and green beer, including photos with 'Not Guilty' Adams fans wearing green t-shirts with my name and logo.

5. Viewing police videos of clients arrested on DUIs and brainstorming on strategies to create reasonable doubt.

6. Steve's annual elf photo shoots.

7. Office Christmas parties.

8. Listening to Steve's dictations and figuring out what he's trying to say.

9. Impromptu happy hours at Filibusters (my office bar; it's awesome!).

10. Steve's annual seminar "What civil attorneys should know about criminal and DUI defense."

The bottom line is that rarely a day goes by without our staff finding something to laugh about. When someone is in a bad mood, another staff member will rise to the occasion to get everyone to laugh and have a productive, happy day.

The result is that there is an abundance of positive energy in my law office, making it next to impossible to have a bad day.

The Magic of a Firm Retreat

Working in a law office 8 to 12 hours a day can become physically exhausting and claustrophobic. **As your firm leader, it's your job to find a way to break away from the firm routine to refuel and refresh staff energy.**

One great way to do it is a **team retreat,** ideally held at a location far away from the home office even if it is in the same city. This change of scene becomes the backdrop for a rejuvenating experience. Why? Because being together provides an opportunity for recreation and education, and most importantly, a chance to BOND. The staff gets to know one another in a different social context.

Retreats range from little more than tax-deductible vacations to motivational, often inspirational, events. **In planning a retreat, it's essential to have clarity of purpose and detailed planning, so that all in attendance have a great time.**

Some retreats are free form, and totally social, whereas others have a pre-set agenda distributed a week or two prior to the retreat. This allows participants to start thinking about the issues on the agenda.

In any case, **team retreats get you out of the daily routine of business at home, with no phone calls, no client meetings, and no interruptions.** Rather than being weighed down by "work product" for the practice, you can focus on big ideas for the firm. Your complete focus is the agenda that you set forth so that you can engage in mastermind thinking about the issues most relevant to the firm.

- You travel to a great destination and experience something new as a team. If you can't afford to travel then get a private room in a nice restaurant for a day or two.
- We book our own conference room. Typically, I get a hotel suite, with a spectacular view, one that can accommodate as many as six people. Our past retreat sites included Chicago and Las Vegas.

5

- We work and play hard. The goal is to get everyone laughing and bonding.

- Seminars are typically one-and-a half to two days.

- We focus on unique issues that we need to think about in detail. Everybody has input. We often come up with spectacular ideas.

- We have people assigned to take copious notes so that we can remember the ideas and execute the game plan once we get back to the office.

- After the day is finished, we wine and dine the staff and create fun things to do and experience together.

- Delegation is critical. Once we come up with certain ideas or projects, we assign people to those projects and specify dates for them to come up with the game plan or the answer for the project.

- In past years, our group thinking has focused on the following:

  - We went over the book *17 Indisputable Laws of Teamwork,* by John Maxwell.
  - Bettering communication within the firm and for clients.
  - Social media planning
  - Better customer service
  - Better efficiency within the firm
  - Better delegating within the firm
  - Template letter designs
  - Thinking about and creating systems for the firm
  - Creating our mission and vision statements
  - Better use of technology
  - Respecting the staff's time

- E-book topics
- Planning an upcoming law firm seminar
- Creating a checklist for administrative functions
- Website strategy and social media execution
- Marketing and marketing budgets
- Individual meetings with staff members
- Creating better client surveys
- Sharing calendars better
- Keeping track of client results
- Thoughts on video creation and planning, and creating videos for the website and YouTube.
- Google ads and internet marketing

- The bottom line is that these meetings are awesome for focusing on a particular issue and getting everybody's thoughts, input, and creating ideas. Four to six minds thinking together are better than one.

- The boss pays for everything, and the staff appreciates that your goal is to make sure that everyone has a great time and one that enhances the growth of the firm.

- During the normal course of a chaotic work week, you and your staff will not have time to focus in detail on the above issues.

5

29
The End of the Road

In every office culture there will be times of conflict when staff members need critical guidance or discipline, or as the last resort, termination.

Firing an employee is a tough thing to do. In fact, if possible, I prefer to avoid termination by getting an employee to leave the practice on their own volition, which preserves their dignity and releases me from being the bad guy.

For example, I had a part-time employee, a young woman who worked as a bookkeeper at a corporate firm in Cincinnati. Her job at our firm was to monitor monthly cash flow, pay our bills, and create projections for our overall operating costs. She happened to be pregnant and overwhelmed, as it turns out, by both her full-time job and her work for me.

We got to a point, unfortunately, where some of our bills were not being paid at all! When I spoke to her, I could tell that she was distracted and that her primary concern was NOT working for me. Because I liked her, I didn't want to just fire her, so I asked her a series of questions about how she was going to accomplish her work and still take care of personal matters. She came to the conclusion that she just couldn't fulfill her duties, and she decided to leave on her own. Because I handled her with respect, she agreed to leave and to even help me find someone to fill the position. It was a win-win.

There are, however, cases where an employee must be terminated, whether or not you want to do it. And you, as the leader, must have the skill set to have that hard conversation and to deliver the unvarnished truth with care and respect.

Rather than feeling guilty when firing someone, view it this way... **you're allowing them the freedom to find a position better suited to them.** Terminating them with that mindset, it's even possible to instill in a person the excitement that comes from anticipating a new adventure.

In any case, **avoidance of termination for cause is not an option.** Your failure to fire will have a detrimental effect on your leadership, your business, and on the morale of other employees. **So it must be done for the higher good of the practice.**

In all cases, before firing anyone, you must talk with them first, giving them a warning, and the chance to improve their performance.

Your focus should be on clarifying the problem:
- ✓ Do it privately, not publicly, avoid shaming someone
- ✓ Have another trusted employee present
- ✓ Do it promptly, so the issue doesn't linger
- ✓ Be polite and respectful, no belittlement or sarcasm
- ✓ Start with a compliment about the things they do right
- ✓ Then focus on one issue at a time
- ✓ Avoid words like "always" and "never"
- ✓ Present criticisms, not attacks
- ✓ Make your point once and don't keep repeating it
- ✓ Deal only with subjects a person can change
- ✓ Criticize the conduct, not the person
- ✓ Make sure they understand your points
- ✓ Listen with care to their response

✓ Do not demonstrate favoritism
✓ Do not apologize for initiating the conference
✓ Afterward, recognize and appreciate improvements

In the worst-case scenario, you will be called upon to terminate a staff member. This can be for a variety of reasons: [32]

- Inadequate performance (chronic failure to produce quality work).
- Refusal to follow directions, e.g., insubordination.
- Dishonesty
  - Cheating on expense accounts
  - Stealing postage stamps, supplies, or anything else
  - Breaking the law
  - Tarnishing your practice's reputation/brand image
  - Doing personal work at the office
  - Hiding client information from the practice
- Inconsistency and unreliability
- Drug or alcohol abuse
- Tardiness or high absenteeism
- Inability to work harmoniously with other employees
- Mediocrity or lack of ambition
- Lack of self-discipline
- Procrastination
- Lack of concentration
- Lack of enthusiasm
- Intolerance or close-mindedness
- Egotism and vanity
- Excuse-making
- Passing the buck and blaming others for one's mistakes
- Lack of organization
- Infecting the company culture with a negative attitude

---

32 https://www.thebalance.com/top-reasons-for-getting-fired-2060732

- Being repeatedly rude or disrespectful to clients or coworkers, after a previous reprimand and fair warning.
- Not delivering work product on deadline

CONCLUSION: If one or more of these reasons leads you to a decision to terminate, get all your ducks in a row:

- Consult with your attorney to discuss reasons for the termination.
- Do it in a private meeting with one witness present to avoid the risk of an employee later claiming you said things you did not.
- Be objective, professional, and keep it simple. Briefly explain, but don't over-explain, the reason for firing.
- Do it calmly, with respect and care.
- Thank them for their contributions.
- Never argue (no matter what the reaction of the employee, don't get sucked into an argument).
- Don't offer to help when you can't.
- Retrieve office property and change all passwords for access.
- Handle the paperwork
  - Explain when he or she will receive the last paycheck
  - Review what happens to benefits, health, severance
- **Tie up the loose ends**
  - Do they work the rest of the day or leave immediately?
  - When can they collect their belongings?
  - Do their coworkers know this is happening?
  - What should they tell clients?
  - What should they do about appointments scheduled for the rest of the week?

For additional resources visit the Ironman Resource page at www.PracticeLawLikeAnIronman.com/resources

PART SIX

BECOMING THE "PURPLE COW"

Branding, Marketing, and Content-Building

30

Distinguishing Yourself from the Herd

> *"Your brand is what other people say about you when you're not in the room!"*
>
> – Jeff Bezos –

Now that you have your office set up—client services and fees established and staff support in place—**you're ready to focus on the branding and marketing of your firm.**

The goal is being **creative**, **consistent**, and, above all, **memorable**, finding innovative ways to capture the public attention, acquire new clients, and grow revenue.

> *You must lead with your true difference, the quality of your experience and personality that makes your solo practice unique.*

What separates you from your competitors? **What's the one true thing you stand for?** *This* is the trait that must be marketed, one that will propel your reputation building, voice, and messaging.

So how *can* you stand out from the competition?

It's all about BRANDING, a technique of defining your business to yourself, to your team, and to your client base.

This is your **business "identity,"** epitomizing the core of what your law practice is all about, its mission and values.

In today's digital culture of the internet and social media, expert personal branding is just as essential as your law degree. It's career survival.

It consists of these five elements:

- ✓ **THE LOGO** (the visual emblem that captures the eye).
- ✓ **THE PRODUCT** (your education, expertise, proven record).
- ✓ **THE PACKAGE** (your conventional and social media presence).
- ✓ **THE PROCESS** (how your practice works, what it accomplishes).
- ✓ **THE PEOPLE** (your staff, dedicated to superior client service).

When potential clients connect with your brand, it's because they share the same values and beliefs. That shared vision leads to higher sales and better brand differentiation. It also leads to loyalty and repeat business.

Above all, branding is the art of self-marketing, so promote your solo practice as a complete package.

6 In the formulation of your brand:

- ✓ Narrow your focus to your ideal client's unmet needs.
- ✓ Define problems the customers don't know they have.
- ✓ Give customers a way to collaborate and personalize their interactions.
- ✓ Imbue everything you do with a higher purpose, rather than connected to sales and money.

REMEMBER, *you're selling not only your expertise as an attorney, but the image you present to the public, through your physical presentation, right down to how you carry yourself.*

* * * * *

Once you define your brand, i.e., your distinctive difference, you need to capture and communicate it in a simple, bold way.

In my view, you have to be daring. **Be a maverick. Outthink the competition.** That's the motto of marketing guru Seth Godin, the author of *Purple Cow: Transform Your Business by Being Remarkable,* one of the inspirations for writing this book.

His overriding theme is that the *key to success is finding a way to STAND OUT, to be the purple cow in a field of monochrome Holsteins.*

We all know that a herd of cattle (just like a herd of monotonous law firms) all look alike. They blend in together. They deaden the eye.

You need to be that law firm that draws in clients like a magnet with word-of-mouth referrals. Your practice offers something irresistible that's worth getting the business it deserves.

Once you've established a reputation as a unique "flavor," the challenge is to do two things simultaneously, as **SETH GODIN** summarizes in his landmark book: [33]

- "Milk the cow for everything it's worth (figure out how to extend it and profit from it for as long as possible)."

---

[33] https://www.fastcompany.com/46049/praise-purple-cow

- "Create a strategy to invent a new purple cow in time to replace the first one, when its benefits inevitably trail off."

REMEMBER: *Almost everything you <u>don't</u> do is a result of fear or inertia or a historical lack of someone asking, "Why not?"*

SO BE THE PURPLE COW. As GODIN says in his book, *"Vanilla is a compromise ice cream flavor, while habanero pecan is not!"*

When branding my own image as a Cincinnati-based DUI defense attorney, I advertise an indefatigable work ethic, which ultimately leads to a *not guilty* verdict (or at least a very good plea bargain).

My work motto is all about **passion**, **persistence**, **resilience**, **dedication**, and **determination**, values I learned during my years competing in the Ironman Triathlon.

To me, these traits are the keys to getting outstanding outcomes in the courtroom, which makes me a formidable adversary.

Clients know that I actually give a damn, that I care about the outcome of their cases, and that I'll work harder than anyone to get a favorable outcome.

That's often the difference between a solo practitioner and an institutional practitioner. As learned during the nine years I worked in a county prosecutor's office, not many government attorneys work longer than a 40-hour week to extend themselves to clients and enhance their skills as attorneys. But, in trying hundreds of cases and hundreds of pre-trial motions over my 26-year career, I've learned that to achieve "not guilty" verdicts and outstanding plea agreements, 40 hours won't do it.

And even when it doesn't seem as if a case can possibly result in a not *guilty* outcome, I'm still willing to give it a shot, underlining that I will work relentlessly to achieve positive results.

That's my *brand*, conveying confidence in my ability to argue a case and persuade jurors and judges to make a finding of *not guilty*.

It's a theme played out in all my advertising and logo positioning: I stamp my practice with words like *liberty* and *justice*, which is why I use an image of the Statue of Liberty for my firm logo and why I branded my website NotGuiltyAdams.com. In this country you are presumed innocent not "guilty"! All in all, my promise is to zealously defend my clients in order to reveal any reasonable doubt leading to a not guilty verdict or a successful outcome thru a negotiated plea that is fair and just, under the circumstances.

For me, marketing is the fun part of being a lawyer, an opportunity to **advertise**, **network**, and **promote** a solo practice by using language and images that appeal to potential clients. And here's one of my favorite ways to do it.

THE POWER OF YOUR STORY

6

Personality is a crucial factor in your branding, generating avid interest from both the media and potential clients. Equal to your skill as a lawyer, it's your primary calling card, a trait that will determine your success above all others.

In other words, how you relate to people is key. You must project a likeable, approachable persona. It's what you say and how you say it that counts. In fact, without even speaking, you must convey a professional, highly competent presence that enhances your brand.

Sure, you're selling your **legal strengths** and **problem-solving abilities**. But you're also selling your **people skills** and your likeability, in the courts, at the office, and in interaction with clients.

And one essential ingredient of personality is the art of storytelling, sharing anecdotes and life experiences that demonstrate your unique talents and perspective. This is telling a client your story in an open, honest, and entertaining way. This story builds trust, fosters openness, and reveals what drives you to make a difference for customers.

Why is this so important? Because the implementation of stories: [34]

- ✓ Creates emotion and builds trust.
- ✓ Paints a picture of where your business is headed.
- ✓ Reveals shared lessons, exposing your human side.
- ✓ Reinforces your firm's values and vision of its future.
- ✓ Extends your appeal to a clearly defined ideal client.
- ✓ Frames a message that addresses their needs.
- ✓ Draws customers into a story that resonates with their life experience.

6 What IS your story? What unique anecdotes can you share about you and your company? The stories you choose should convey:

- Who you are
- Why you do what you do
- What keeps you energized and committed

34 https://www.krusecontrolinc.com/power-of-storytelling-to-connect-trust-close-sales/

- What keeps you awake at night
- What motivates, thrills, and scares you
- What makes you laugh
- What you are doing to make this a better world

Do <u>not</u> give clients or staff a chronological history of your company. Instead talk about:

- The moment you came face-to-face with the biggest, most audacious idea that you ever had, and charged right in.
- What was missing in the world until you created your big idea.
- Yourself as a kid and your self-image as a lawyer.
- How you have created a company around passion.
- Get your story down to a concise sound bite.

So tell a story about...

- A legal victory that will resonate with prospective clients.
- Employee dedication to your firm's customer service.
- Focus on giving each client top value and service.
- Present testimonials (a subject we'll cover in depth).
- The mission of your firm.
- The things you can do as an attorney better than anyone.
- A unique trend in your area of practice.
- How emotionally connected you are to clients.
- An out-of-the-office fun or creative pursuit.

6

REMEMBER, *your story is paramount because it reflects your passion, purpose, values, and personality.*

If you want to take a giant step forward in marketing your practice, you can also flip the exchange of storytelling. Invite your clients and prospects to share with you, drawing them in as collaborative partners. As John Jantsch suggests in his book *The Commitment Engine: Making Work Worth It,* ask them:

- **What do you know about your niche that nobody else does?**
- **What is your firm's greatest defect?**
- **If your firm could choose a new identity, what would it be?**
- **What is your favorite customer story?**
- **What is your secret wish for your business?**
- **What is the greatest challenge your business must overcome?**
- **What is your greatest fear?**
- **What is your greatest achievement? Disappointment?**
- **What event of your childhood shaped your destiny?**
- **What choices have you made that you regret?**

It may take some guts to pose questions like this to your best clients, but when you do it, you'll be on your way to building a relationship that cannot be penetrated by competitors.

6 SLOGANS WORK!

One of the best (and least expensive) ways to brand your practice is by using a law practice **SLOGAN, a handful of strategically selected words that encapsulate everything you stand for, and everything your target clientele needs to know about you.**

It's this slogan, or attorney tagline, that broadcasts your services to the world.

It's amazing how good slogans are a great way to start a conversation …about criminal law, the Constitution, and the government's burden of proof. Good slogans also inform your staff how they should conduct themselves and what makes the firm unique.

Here are a few sample slogans from established law firms:

- Small but Mighty
- The Art of Law
- Low Ball, High Quality
- Bigger is Good. Smarter is Better
- Not If, But How
- Lawyers You'll Swear By
- Everything Matters
- One Firm Worldwide
- Relationships that Drive Results
- We're in This Together. Your Team and Ours
- Aligned for Excellence

But slogans like these are a bit dull. In my criminal and DUI-focused practice, I've created a set of informally entertaining slogans for print, radio and YouTube. I can tell you that a catchy attorney tagline will both inspire your firm and spread the word about it.

In my opinion, many attorneys talk in legalese with taking-themselves-too-seriously-grim expressions. But I've always found that talking in plain English (or even slang) can get the consumer to listen and believe. Instead of being perceived as an elite, arrogant authority figure, you're a genuine, direct, down-to-earth equal. **Big difference.**

The common denominator is plain talk, which allows the potential client to better relate to you.

As a former prosecutor and criminal DUI defense attorney, I freely use the slang of criminal law to make my point. The police, in the jargon of the trade, are known as the *Po Po.* So whenever I'm on a radio show as a guest, I tell listeners to *Say No No to the Po Po,* one of my firm's prime slogans, as defined below.

And thanks to radio ads and appearances, many listeners have told me that they put my name and phone number into their cell phone contacts, in case they ever need me.

All in all, for me, radio advertising has been the second-biggest form of advertising next to word-of-mouth. It's relatively inexpensive and can be pinpointed to your exact geographical market.

In the end, a touch of humor and self-deprecation can do wonders, which is why my firm, as I mentioned earlier, employs more humor than most. I've found that it's always good to work in threes. So I consistently use this set of direct, memorable marketing slogans:

✓ SAY NO-NO TO THE PO-PO!

✓ CHOOSE TO REFUSE!

✓ IF YOU'RE STOPPED BY THE MAN, CALL THE MAN!

6 "Say 'NO NO' TO THE 'PO PO!'"

This directive targeted to Ohio and Kentucky citizens, means that you should **not** consent to be **interviewed**, tested or **interrogated** by the police when stopped on the road. Specifically, you should:

- Refuse field sobriety tests
- Refuse breath testing

- Refuse urine and blood testing
- Refuse polygraph testing
- Refuse DNA testing (unless ordered by a court)
- Refuse consent for the police to search any of your personal belongings, your computers, your house, or your car.
- Refuse to provide a statement
- Note that **advice to refuse is contingent on the crime and/or penalty of refusing, which varies from state to state.**

In this country, the state has and always will have the burden of proof. Therefore, the suspected or accused citizen does not have to aid the government by giving evidence to prove their case.

My "Po-Po" slogan has become so recognizable that wherever I go in Cincinnati, friends in the court and complete strangers around town are always shouting that slogan out to me!

To reinforce the concept behind the slogan, and to market the firm, we've even printed laminated business cards, Solo Cups, Koozies and T-shirts with do's and don'ts. These tips include:

- Produce license, registration and insurance upon request
- Get OUT of the car if asked
- DO NOT answer questions about where or what you've been drinking.
- NO admissions
- NO roadside tests
- No breath, blood, or urine tests
- Remember to remain silent and LAWYER UP
- See www.notguiltyadams.com for more details

6

"CHOOSE TO REFUSE!"

This is another slogan that refers to the same protocol, our directive to refuse any type of chemical test or roadside gymnastic tests that the government seeks to impose on you as it relates to a DUI investigation and/or arrest. **Choose to refuse that government junk science!**

(Note that advice to refuse is contingent on the crime and/or penalty of refusing, which varies from state to state.)

"STOPPED BY THE MAN, CALL THE MAN!"

I always say, "When you're stopped by the Man (Po Po), call the man" (ME!)

For example, when I'm in the courthouse and see police officers walking throughout the hallways, some of them jokingly blurt out "Stopped by the Man," and then I finish the sentence of my advertised slogan by saying "Call the Man!" They get a kick out of it.

"IF YOU'RE THINKING OF LEAVIN', YOU BETTER CALL STEVEN!"

Now that I've expanded my area of practice to include family law, including separation, divorce, and child custody, I'm using a light-hearted slogan. Sure, divorce is a serious issue, but our rationale is that a lighter touch will capture the attention of the potential client, who may be attracted to a friendly vibe.

I use all of these taglines in my YouTube commercials, on my website, in print advertising, and on my firm's customized promotional items, which include:

- T-shirts
- Pens
- Cups
- Koozies (foam sleeves that thermally insulate a beverage)
- Christmas stockings and Santa hats
- Coasters
- Business cards
- Napkins

Armed with marketing slogans of your own, you can network efficiently at seminars and professional events.

I stood up and said, "Hello my name is Steven R. Adams. I'm from Cincinnati, Ohio, home of *Say No No to the Po Po, Choose to Refuse, and If You're Stopped by the Man, Call the Man!* And by the way I am going to crush it!" Everyone laughed, and after that, I got a lot of attention. It was a great opportunity for networking and expanding marketing techniques.

> **REMEMBER:** *Having a law degree and solid experience alone will not make you a sought-after lawyer. Since law school never properly prepares anyone for the art of marketing, you have to actively, yet ethically, promote your practice in whatever ways you can.*

6

I can tell you that legendary attorneys like Alan Dershowitz, Mark Geragos, Gloria Allred, and Gerry Spence, and hundreds of others, are all masters of media exposure, creating their unique brand through proper marketing and promotion.

TESTIMONIALS

Another key element for solo-practice marketing is the astute use of **TESTIMONIALS, positive reviews and comments from satisfied clients presented in text, audio, or video form.** These commendations, usually just a sentence or two, can be featured in your:

- ✓ **COMPANY BROCHURE** and direct mail promotion
- ✓ **WEBSITE** — homepage, separate link, sidebars,
- ✓ **RADIO, TV, INTERNET, AND PRINT ADS**
- ✓ **SOCIAL MEDIA**

A great testimonial is like a short letter of recommendation. And you'll find that most clients will be happy to provide a few written sentences that you can feature in all your marketing campaigns. Though some clients prefer anonymity and will decline your request, most won't. Over time, you'll build an impressive gallery of testimonials.

In the end, testimonials are effective because they:

- Build trust
- Bolster credibility
- Offer proof of your skills
- Overcome skepticism
- Substantiate your claims

6

31
The Marketing Basics

As we've seen, when you brand yourself as unique and use the full power of your personality, you're already well on the way to marketing your way to success.

You're going to be the law firm that provides a breakthrough service that stands out like a neon light. To do that, you need to establish one unique thing about you or your service that gets people talking, "forcing" them to tell others about you.

But how do you get that started?

- **Create a stellar website,** a welcome mat to your practice both visually arresting and fully informative, complete with testimonials, video introduction, firm accomplishments, accreditations, and services provided.

- **Create a portfolio of successes,** the accomplished work you've done in the past, including testimonials from former clients (a subject we'll detail in a moment). All this builds trust.

- **Create a series of memorable slogans** that epitomize your specialty.

- **Create videos** for both your website and YouTube.

- **Create a Firm Marketing Kit.**
    - Your case statement (why a client should hire you).

- Your difference summary (your unique approach distinct from the competition).
- Your ideal client/customer description.
- Your marketing story (see storytelling section).
  - ☐ Brochure should include the firm's business card, printed brochure, stationery, all coordinated with your branding logo and theme.

- **Create a LinkedIn profile,** your online resume, cover letter and references document all rolled into one. If people like your work ethic, get them to write a public LinkedIn recommendation.

- **Refine your resume:**
  - Your accomplishments
  - Your community service
  - Your educational background
  - Your mission statement
  - Your law practice information
  - Practice or niche information
  - Contact information
  - Customer service philosophy

- **Attend events:** Legal conventions and conferences are effective ways to build a network and spread your message. Talk about what you do and what separates you from the competition.

- **Build media contacts** for guest appearance interviews.

- **Speak at events,** allowing you to demonstrate your expertise to a larger audience, which will lead to contacts and opportunities:
  - A CLE in your field of practice
  - A professional organization event
  - Any social event is an opportunity
  - Volunteer (opens the door to "sitting next to a stranger")

6

- **Bond with the community:**
  - Attend seminars, trade shows, continuing education, professional organizations
  - Rotary
  - Kiwanis
  - Lions
  - Chamber of Commerce
  - Jaycees (Junior Chamber of Commerce)
  - Churches, temples, schools

- **Write articles** in law journals, magazines, online sites. Consider a blog of your own, a great place to spread your brand. If you don't want to write your own blog, use a service like Lexblog (**www.lexblog.com**).
  - Syndicated to the LXBN.com network, the largest curation of legal blogs
  - Grows the number of people who know your firm
  - Puts your content in front of more than 15,000 followers

- **Stay connected** by doing Google searches for other legal bloggers. Analyze what others are doing to market themselves. Check out these top legal blogs:
  - Myshingle.com
  - Attorneyatwork.com
  - Lawyerist.com
  - Solopracticeuniversityblog.com
  - Legal Loud Speaker Blog
  - Lawpracticetipsblog.com
  - Abovethelaw.com/small-law-firms
  - Loweringthebar.net
  - www.attorneymarketing.com/blog

- www.therainmakerblog.com
- Lawmarketing.com
- www.legalproductivity.com
- Sololawyerbydesign.com
- www.lawsiteblog.com
- www.smallfirminnovation.com
- www.mycase.com/blog
- Mylawlicense.blogspot.com
- Above the Law
- Scotusblog
- ABA Journal/The Lawyer's Magazine
- Canna Law Blog
- The Fashion Law
- Law and Liberty
- Law Technology Today
- The Crime Report

- **Advertising**
  - Print
  - TV
  - Radio
  - Internet (LinkedIn, Facebook)
  - Google Ad words
  - Pay per click

- **Selectively use social media:** Twitter, Facebook, YouTube, Pinterest, Google, Tumblr, Instagram
  - Follow wisely
  - Read what others have to say and respond appropriately
  - Map prospects and customers
  - Build lists
  - Share daily

- Share other people's content
- Use search function to find prospects

- **Create content that builds trust**
  - Post customer reviews on sites such as Yelp and AVVO
  - Post testimonials and endorsements from satisfied customers and colleagues who can speak authoritatively
  - Post articles written by you in publications

- **Design content that educates**
  - Produce ad and brochure copy
    - ☐ Describe your unique approach
    - ☐ Tell your firm's history
  - Conduct seminars, in person or online
  - Produce video success stories
  - Provide customer- or industry-specific feeds produced by others that may help your client base

REMEMBER: *Your brand will be reflected:*

- **INTERNALLY:**
  - Business cards
  - Letterhead
  - Envelopes
  - Firm brochures
  - Invoices

- **EXTERNALLY:**
  - Advertising
  - Promotional campaigns
  - Website

It's all these components, blended together, that result in your being accessible and distinctive — so useful and noteworthy that your market listens to what you have to say.

WEBSITE

Short of being able to speak to someone directly, your website is the most important marketing tool you have. Many of your prospects will first "meet" you on your website. **So it's essential that its pages:**

- ✓ Reflect the essence of the firm, its mission and brand.
- ✓ Match the firm's marketing materials
- ✓ Be visually appealing and user friendly, easy to navigate.
- ✓ Be well-written and concise
- ✓ Be mobile-friendly to all portable devices
- ✓ Include an optional audio, maybe a welcome message or a guide (www.audioAcrobat.com) .
- ✓ Where possible, be interactive - create a Q&A with likely questions from potential clients about your practice.

In designing your solo law firm website, avoid these MISTAKES[35]

- ▪ Speaking in legalese.
- ▪ Websites that look like copycat templates.
- ▪ Going overboard on lawyer stock images (photos of gavels, courthouses).
- ▪ Lack of compliance with attorney advertising, disclaimers, and ethics:

---

35 https://jurispage.com/2013/seo/7-website-mistakes-law-firms-make/ https://blog.lexicata.com/6-pitfalls-law-firm-website/

- Look up your state's legal ethics rules as they apply to attorney advertising.
- Add the necessary disclosures required by the ethics rules.
- Remove any content from your website that violates these rules.

- **Lack of Search Engine Optimization.** Your web site may look cosmetically great, but potential clients may be unable to find you, so hire a third-party SEO consulting company.

- **Outdated content.** Avoid by placing most current blogs, published articles, print, video, or radio interviews on the site first.

REMEMBER: *Law-firm websites today must be designed for maximum visitor involvement and client conversion opportunities, while maximizing search engine visibility. (You may also want to create an app for your firm, which allows potential customers to analyze data about it).*

So, HIRE AN EXPERT! This is not a do-it-yourself project. The mission of your web designer is:

- Develop an overall <u>theme</u> that matches the firm's brand/image
- Domain name — be inventive without violating state bar rules.
- Produce a clean professional design.
- Include a concise personal biography and a description of your firm's mission.
- Provide links to your speeches, videos, publications.
- Provide astute keyword identification (for search engine optimization purposes):
  - Google Ad words
  - MOZ.com

6

- SEMRush.com
- Wordtracker.com

- **Ranking Tools:**
  - Moz.com
  - SEMRush
  - WebCEO
  - Rankchecker.com
- **Develop content (in the form of copy, video, slide shows).**
- **HTML coding and tagging.**
- **Ensure secure hosting and domain registration.**
- **Establish a system for search engine optimization.**
- **Advertise on Avvo.com; Superlawyers.com; Bestlawyers.com.**
- **Create a landing page for promotion of free video course, E-book, newsletter subscription, free tips report.**
- **Create an auto-responder to routine inquiries, which allows you to capture leads. But do not bombard your new subscriber with sales copy.**
- **Create signature videos:**
  - An introductory video should be dignified, professional, and focused on what your firm can do for a client.
  - Be congenial, warm, and exhibit a sense of humor.
  - Use storytelling as a way to engage the viewer ("When I was growing up, my dad was a lawyer and always told me…").
  - See: www.REELSCO.com, a viable online video marketing resource.

To find great web developers, mobile developers, designers, and writers, consult Upwork.com, Web.com, Elance.com, Odesk.com.

CREATING A POWER BIOGRAPHY

- **Create Your Profile on Facebook, LinkedIn, Google, Twitter. Consider added profiles on Pinterest, Instagram, Reddit, Quora:**[36]

  - Hire a photographer to capture a professional headshot (with a friendly natural expression — smile, half-smile, or thoughtful).

  - As Jon Jantsch recommends in *Duct Tape Marketing: The World's Most Practical Small Business Marketing Guide*, use Vizify and About.me to build profile pages by drawing images already used in social media.

    - ☐ Feature short stories and succinct comments rather than résumé-laden postings. Use an active first-person voice.

    - ☐ Focus on where you have been, what you've learned.

    - ☐ Post media interviews and articles published.

    - ☐ Talk about your passions, hobbies, sports (but no politics or religion).

    - ☐ Link your company website to your social media profile.

    - ☐ Use KnowEm to instantly check the use of your brand, product, personal name, or username on over 500 popular social networks.

6

---

36 https://www.ducttapemarketing.com/social-profile/

BLOGS

A blog is a short article written by you (or someone you hire) that will:

- ✓ Inexpensively increase your search engine visibility
- ✓ Demonstrate your legal expertise

Both benefits can help attract more clients. A good blog generates opinions from fellow lawyers, clients, and/or journalists. Your posting tells the reader something about your business and passion, something you have observed that interests you, or something you have learned and can't wait to share.

As valuable as a blog can be in the digital age, few lawyers take advantage of it. In fact, according to the American Bar Association, only two percent of lawyers blog!

This number will no doubt increase as social media becomes more and more integrated into the orbit of a law practice. As John Jantsch suggests in *Duct Tape Selling: Think Like a Marketer — Sell Like a Superstar: :*

- ■ **Choose a domain** name that's consistent with your practice, such as NewYorkTrafficTicketLawyer.com, or my own: JumpStartYourLawPractice.com.

- ■ **Choose a host:** the most popular blogware is WordPress (www.wordpress.org) or Google's Blogger (www.blogger.com).

- ■ **Content:** Create content that is both informative and interesting. It's not what you know, it's how you say it. Your writing needs to display your personality and humanity. Ask questions, seek opinions.

- **Frequency:** At the beginning, you should post four or five items a week (not on weekends), eventually publishing two to three times weekly. You don't need to be a writer, just write like you SPEAK.

- **Length:** Start with 300-500 words, unless your topic is highly technical and needs elaborate explanation.

- **Tags and categories:** To keep your posts organized, create a category for the main topics covered. Use tags to alert readers to hot topics.

- **Add plug-ins:** Sites like WPbeginner.com offer advice on configuration of plug-ins. Consider adding a subscribed comments plug-in so people get an email notice when someone responds to their comment.

- **Title bar:** There's no substitute for an attention-grabbing headline, with a visual image that draws people in.

- **Link to others:** To draw readers in, you need to link your blog to other bloggers and websites. This will increase organic searches on Google, Bing, and other search engines. So try to engage bloggers in conversation.

- **Make blog accessible in multiple formats:** Programs like Feedblitz.com allow readers to receive blog posts by email, while you can package blog posts into an e-book that you can make available for download at your website.

- **Subscribe to blogs of competitors.**

- **Use analytics:** Make sure that your blog grows by keeping track of statistics through an analytics package: (www. google.com/analytics) or Site Meter.

- **www.sitemeter.com.** This way you can keep track of the number of visitors to your site and find out what search terms or word combinations are drawing readers in:

  - The more frequently the blog is updated, the higher the rank

6

- Be included in directories of fellow lawyers
- Use RebelMouse, aggregating all your sharing activity to a single page, including your tweets, pins, and shares

- **Spread the word!** Send out a link to your blog to your entire mailing list, including clients, friends, family, and colleagues, and consider polling clients to find out what they would like to read in a blog.

- **Introduce new hires** with a rounded portrait of their experience.

TOP PODCASTING TIPS

A PODCAST **is a series of audio or video media files that are released episodically and downloaded through web syndication, like iTunes.** It's like having a radio show of your own, which you record and edit in advance. You then release it on the internet (instead of on the radio). Refer to such model podcasts as: **Lawyer2Lawyer, Rocket Lawyer, Duct Tape marketing podcast, Legal Lad Quick, and Dirty Tips for a More Lawful Life.**

Podcasting is a powerful marketing tool. Its audio content is accessible on any smartphone or portable device. You can interview leading experts in your field, current or former clients, members of your strategic network, or leading authors and industry experts. All you need is a microphone, a computer, and a low-cost phone service like Skype, plus the right software.

Having a podcast can also open doors for books, public speaking, and jobs, and it's a great technique for creating your unique niche. Ideally, you should release a new episode every week, on the same day. Your listeners will expect it and look forward to it.

Don't forget to invest in a quality microphone and headphones to create the best sound possible. Think of the podcast as a hobby, not a money-making venture.

As **JOHN JANTSCH** recommends in his book *Duct Tape Selling: Think Like A Marketer-Sell Like A Superstar:*

- Choose a length that allows you to meaningfully cover a topic but that leaves listeners wanting more. I recommend 20 minutes.

- Aim for consistency in the length of your podcast so listeners know what to expect.

- Register your podcast in iTunes, as that's where 90 percent of them are heard.

- Subscribe to podcasts:
  - John Jantsch's *Duct Tape Selling: Think Like a Marketer— Sell Like a Superstar* Podcast
  - John Jantsch's *EO Fire Podcast* (Entrepreneur on Fire)
  - Seth Godin's *Startup School*
  - Michael Stelzner's *The Social Media Marketing Podcast on Social Media Examiner*
  - Chris Brogan's *The Human Business Way*
  - *The Advanced Selling Podcast*
  - Michael Hyatt's *This Is Your Life*
  - Pat Flynn's *Smart Passive Incomes*

6

BUSINESS CARDS

While your website and profiles on LinkedIn or, FindLaw and AVVO connect you to the digital world, your **business card is essential too.** Sure, it's old school, but an impeccably printed business card is still essential for one-on-one social interactions in the physical world.

So always **carry cards** with you and attach them to every written document sent out by your office (and consider developing a **firm brochure** that features a tear-off business card for potential clients as well). When it comes to business cards:

- **Keep it simple** — nothing with flashy images or wild fonts.
- **Keep it relevant** — your name, phone number(s), email, physical address and website are essential, social media tags optional.
- **Convey your brand** — show your style by the weight and feel of the card, engrave it, use a company logo, and use color.
- **Make it unique** — consider folding cards that have a slogan or tips on the back, but avoid 3D elements, glitter, exotic fabrics.
- **Make it memorable** — something clients and referral sources will want to keep.

6

NEWSLETTERS

Law firm newsletters are powerfully effective marketing tools, **offering useful, valuable content that capture your unique viewpoint and expertise.** They are a fantastic way to communicate with current and prospective clients, referral sources, colleagues, local businesses, and the media. For optimum exposure, it's most effective to publish consistently, preferably monthly. But whether your newsletter is published monthly or quarterly, it should reflect insightfully on your area of specialty, while also including some personal or community commentary.

Some attorneys hire a legal writing service or a newsletter publisher to create a newsletter, while others do it in-house.

Either way, lawyers should consider these tips for an effective law firm newsletter:

- **Write it in plain English** to capture your personality and natural voice. It should not sound like a court opinion or legal treatise.

- **Use an attention-grabbing HEADLINE** that compels readers to open it up.

- **Use a table of contents** so readers can scan to find subjects that interest them.

- **Concentrate on your most interesting cases** and what you learned (and don't be afraid to be controversial. This is your showcase).

- **Create an attractive graphic template** with unified design elements, typestyles, layout (also consider boxes and photos).

- **Publish something useful,** about broad issues that directly affect your clients.

- **Include articles** from other lawyers in your practice area.

- Include a **relevant book review or report on a seminar** event.

- **Emphasize substance over sales hype** — don't overuse testimonials or hard sell.

- **Invite readers to contact the firm** with prominently displayed information.

- **Mail the newsletter,** using an E-version as a supplement.

6

- **Attach** a newsletter with client information packages.
- **Send** the firm's newsletter to local media and local businesses.
- **Include information about staff,** sharing news about activities, pets, even recipes. Make it fun.
- **Talk** about sports, business, education.
- **Congratulate staff and clients** for accolades they receive.
- **Reference videos** posted on your website or YouTube.
- **Talk about nuances** in legislation, regulations, or the law that may affect your clients or prospective clients.

WHITE PAPERS

Another marketing and business tool, a white paper is an authoritative, persuasive, mini-report used to develop business leads.

Some are short, motivated with a "why you should hire us" theme, and others are in-depth looks at industry trends. All of them seek to address a complex issue while advocating for a solution.

In general, white papers are:
- Approximately six pages
- Published with:
  - Title page
  - Table of contents
  - Executive summary
  - Body
  - Conclusion

- Messaging focused on one subject
- Written in the first or third person, your choice
- Stories and quotations from clients
- Relevant images
- Charts
- Graphics
- Statistics to back up claim

Do you need to write a white paper?

If you're a plaintiff's-side personal injury lawyer, most of your clients aren't going to read a white paper. **But corporate clients will be interested.**

All in all, white papers are <u>targeted</u> to **potential client prospects, referral sources, and other colleagues.**

In addition to a white paper, you can also create:

- E-books
- Free reports
- How-to guides
- Case studies
- Tip sheets
- Trend reports

In a white paper, sprinkle in stories and quotations from clients. Use relevant images, charts, graphics, and detailed statistics to back up any claim made. After you've written enough white papers, you can turn them into a seminar or book.

PRACTICE-AREA PUBLICATION ARTICLES

Write an article for a practice-area publication available in your local community or state, or on a national basis, as recommended in *The Lawyer's Guide to Marketing Your Practice,* by James Durham and Deborah McMurray:

- **Publish in an industry trade publication, one released to other businesses, not just lawyers.**
- **Your article could:**
  - Provide a new perspective on an old problem.
  - Offer words of caution based upon practice experience.
  - Introduce a local take on a national issue.
  - Show a new trend in the law.
- **When writing an article for publication:**
  - Avoid legalese, speak in plain English.
  - Write for an inclusive audience, not just lawyers.
  - Write a paper that you can adapt for speaking engagements, seminars, or an E-book.
  - Do **not** use footnotes.
  - Talk **to** your readers, not about them.
  - Keep your articles between 1,200 and 1,500 words.
- **Once the article is published:**
  - Insert the link on your social media sites and website.
  - Include a print-out in information packets mailed to clients with a business card that says, "With my compliments."

6

TWO-STEP RESPONSE ADVERTISING

As John Jantsch explains in his book *Duct Tape Marketing: The World's Most Practical Small Business Marketing Guide,* two-step response advertising is a marketing technique that motivates a potential client to take a preliminary action, which then allows you to begin marketing directly to them. Whether advertising in newspapers, magazines, radio, TV, or online, the purpose is not so much to "sell" but to generate a list of qualified leads — people who may be inclined to do business with you in the future. Most importantly, **it gives you permission to market to them.** This method eliminates the need for cold calling.

It's a two-step, cost-effective, and efficient process:

<u>Step One:</u> Create a free information product — a report, course, tip sheet, workshop, roundtable, checklist, newsletter, or video. Put your advertising dollars to work and use internet and print ads, direct mail, back of your business card copy, letterhead, email signature, or website to focus on getting people to pick up, request, or download that report. Don't try to do anything else with your advertising, let the report sell you.

Note: People who have requested your free information are officially a hot lead, identifying themselves as someone drawn to what you do. So half of your sales job is already done.

<u>Step Two:</u> Send the report or sample to all those who respond and initiate direct marketing appropriately, with follow-up email, personal note, or newsletter, etc.

This approach is effective because you demonstrate your knowledge and experience in your field of practice in a non-threatening way. You will be building a database of potential clients who may eventually develop as full-fledged clients. **Offer them valuable information.**

6

REMEMBER:

> Create a compelling headline
>
> Articulate the value in the information product
>
> Use testimonial quotes from satisfied clients
>
> Offer your free information or product
>
> Create a call to action, a reason for the reader to respond
>
> Make it easy for them to contact you
>
> Give them the option to visit a webpage or call a toll-free number
>
> Be sure to check your state bar disciplinary rules on advertising. You may have to label the report or free information products as "advertisement only." Check your state rules.

MEDIA KITS

Positive media coverage boosts the confidence of your existing clients and strategic partners and provides them with tangible proof that your firm is a bona fide winner. As John Jantsch summarizes in *Duct Tape Marketing:*

The first step in attracting media coverage is creating a **MEDIA KIT, an organized presentation that introduces your firm, its accomplishments, and hard-breaking news.** It can be presented to any news outlet in either digital form or in hard copy delivered in an attractive binder or folder.

6

The Media Kit:

- Describes you and your firm to reporters, editors, and producers.

- Contains a package of comprehensive information to aid journalists to write stories and should contain:

- Firm brochure
- Firm history
- Firm leadership and staff biographies
- Firm news — press releases and media mentions
  - ☐ Press release is the workhorse of your PR program
  - ☐ Its purpose is to grab the attention of the reporter
  - ☐ Keep it to one page
  - ☐ Focus on ONE subject or news item
  - ☐ Hire an experienced PR expert to write it
  - ☐ Create an attention-grabbing headline. Ninety percent of advertising effectiveness depends upon the headline
  - ☐ Weave your credentials into the press release
- **Facts and figures about area of practice, including brief outlines of recent case wins**
- **White papers, newsletters**
- **Business card**
- **Firm logos**
- **Firm phone numbers**
- **Photos and graphics**
  - Include a recent professional headshot, a 5" x 7" black and white print or high quality digital photo

Once you have your media kit in hand, you'll need a comprehensive list of who to send it to:

- **Create or buy a database of media contacts**
  - ✓ Agilitypr.com
  - ✓ Bitesizepr.com
  - ✓ Cision.com
  - ✓ Mediacontactspro.com

Tips on relating to journalists:

- Identify journalists who cover your niche
- Brief yourself by reading their work
- Follow them on social media
- Research their blogs or online columns
- Subscribe to and comment on their writing
- Create a standard pitch letter that introduces your firm
- Research stories featuring your area of practice
- Invite reporter to meet you in your office
- Establish rapport by asking questions about their background
- Go into the interview with three key message points
- Proactively convey your company's core message
- Avoid legalese, speak in memorable 20-second sound bites
- Allow the reporter to ask questions and guide the discussion
- If you can't answer a question, promise to get the information
- Speak on the record and address only the questions asked
- End the interview with a summarized takeaway message
- Respect their deadlines and respond promptly to queries
- Avoid speaking about other lawyers
- Do not use the phrase "no comment"
- Give the reporter helpful leads and sources

Compile your own list of local publications, and the reporters who cover your industry, easily available on their websites.

6

Add to your list:

- Chamber of Commerce
- Trade associations
- Clubs
- Universities

SPEAKING ENGAGEMENTS

As recommended in *The Lawyer's Guide to Marketing Your Practice*, by James Durham and Deborah McMurray and in *The Referral Engine: Teaching Your Business to Market Itself* by John Jantsch:

- Make it a goal to create two presentations a year, live or a web conference.
- Develop a series of educational talks and/or workshops for business owners, potential clients.
- Present information on a hot topic related to your area of practice.
- Meet audience members before speech to personalize or edit your approach.
- Prepare a one-page handout with your contact information.
- Prepare a written introduction about yourself for the hosts.
- Prepare bullet-point notes, but DON'T read from a script.
  - Practice your talk in advance:
    - ☐ Who is your audience?
    - ☐ Why are they there?
    - ☐ What are they most interested in?

6

- What detail can you give that makes that one thing visual, alive, relevant?
- Why should they care about it?
- Talk about the impact of that one thing in the first two minutes of your speech.
- Memorize introductory and closing sound bites.

- Record your speech in advance to identify strengths, content, delivery.

- Join Toastmasters International to observe other speakers.

- Use a large font, 20 point or more for easy visibility.

- Underline key points in yellow.

- Interweave metaphors, analogies, stories, and quotes.

- Don't worry about how you look or how you sound. BE YOU.

- Use audiovisual equipment to boost interest and meaning.

- Motivate audience participation; ask questions, stimulate discussion. Remember: the best speaker is someone with finely honed listening and relational skills.

- If you use PowerPoint, offer to email your presentation to attendees.

- Don't overstay your welcome, or test audience attention (keep it short!) .

- Invite listeners to sign up for your newsletter (while collecting their business cards).

- Consider joint-venture speaking engagements with noncompeting lawyer.

- **Waive your speaking fee to advertise your practice.**
- **Provide a list of tips to audience members.**
- **Use your firm's slogans.**
- **Offer a free resource guide related to your topic or a more detailed report.**

- Follow up with a handwritten note.
- Prepare an audience survey to provide instant feedback.

Once you've established yourself as an expert in your area of practice, you can consider **hosting workshops** for other attorneys, clients, and colleagues. These will build your exposure and raise your status as a leader in your field.

For public-interest lawyers

Working for low-income clients on the social margins can be exhausting. Burnout and "compassion fatigue" are real risks even for the most dedicated and seasoned attorneys. Your workshop can help identify the causes of burnout, explore participants' own stresses, and acquire skills and perspectives to stay balanced, energized, and creative.

For the private bar

The lives of solo-practice attorneys are filled with multiple stresses and competing demands. Increasingly, lawyers feel the pinch between being productive at work and maintaining physical health, family life, and recreational interests. Proactively addressing work/life balance issues is another fertile area for a possible workshop or retreat.

In addition, you can host or agree to speak at a seminar, conference or workshop in order to teach and instruct lawyers in your field of practice, and give tips, techniques and strategies in handling cases specific to your niche.

6

CONFERENCES

- **LegalTech** (legalweekshow.com): The largest legal technology event of the year, a must-attend. Will enable you to procure practical information for improving your law practice management and technology.

- **ABA Techshow** (techshow.com): More a law-practice management conference than technology-related, with multiple vendors competing for the attention of solo- to mid-size firm lawyers. Exhibit hall vendors are varied and include marketing, credit card processing, and remote receptionist services companies.

- **The Clio Cloud Conference** (eventbrite.com/e/clio-cloud-conference): Focused on innovation and the future of the law.

- **EvolveLaw** (evolvelawnow.com): Designed to connect the legal and tech communities.

WEB CONFERENCES

Live conferences held over the internet are an efficient, convenient way to draw in participants from around the world.

This interactive technology allows real-time sharing of computer screens, on two or more computers or mobile devices.

These so-called **"Webinars"** may be used for peer-level meetings or classes/ workshops to educate any segment of your practice. It's an ideal opportunity to discuss with peers occupational challenges, trends, and approaches in your niche.

Bells and whistles include:
- Slideshow presentations
- Live or streaming video
- VoIP—real time audio communication

- Whiteboard, highlight items on the slide presentation
- Text chat, for live question and answer sessions
- Polls and surveys (surveygizmo.com)
- Screen sharing

ROUNDTABLE DISCUSSIONS

A roundtable is a gathering of about a dozen people, often with similar interests. It's a session that lasts about 90 minutes and is held in your office conference room or at a small space that can be rented at a local hotel or meeting hall.

A well-run roundtable must have:

- ✓ Clear focus
- ✓ Comprehensive agenda
- ✓ Strong moderator — someone articulate, confident, and knowledgeable
- ✓ Select invitation list

Roundtable topics could include:

- Personal Finance for Young Lawyers
- Ethics, Evidence, the Internet and Social Media
- Privatization of Prisons
- Amendments to the Federal Rules of Civil Procedure
- Nuts and Bolts of Class Actions for Young Attorneys
- Blogging and Social Media — Increasing Visibility
- When Courts of Law and Public Opinion Collide
- Rainmakers Share Tips on Increasing Your Book of Business

Be sure to have the roundtable discussion transcribed, as it may be used for a blog, article, or newsletter, or as a link to your website.

32
Down to Business
Your Marketing Budget

So how much is all this going to cost?

According to law firm marketing expert Sally J. Schmidt, **a firm's overall marketing budget should always include the following categories:**

- ✓ Advertising
- ✓ Alumni programs
- ✓ Attendance at industry, trade/professional associations
- ✓ Client entertainment and gifts
- ✓ CRM system or client database
- ✓ Directory listings
- ✓ Events and seminars
- ✓ Graphic design and branding costs
- ✓ Law firm network activities (e.g., membership and travel)
- ✓ Mailings and communications (e.g., newsletters, invitations, announcements, alerts, and holiday cards)
- ✓ Marketing-related training
- ✓ Market research and client surveys
- ✓ Marketing staff professional development

- ✓ Memberships in industry, trade or professional organizations
- ✓ Proposals and pitches
- ✓ Public and media relations
- ✓ Tickets and sponsorships
- ✓ Website design and maintenance

There's a great difference of opinion about what percentage of gross revenues should be spent on firm marketing and advertising. The U.S. Small Business Administration recommends spending 7 to 8 percent of your gross revenue on firm promotion if you're doing less than $5 million a year in sales. But other marketing experts advise that start-ups and small businesses should only allocate between 2 to 3 percent of revenue for promotion. It's really all about what you can afford.

As John Jantsch writes in *Duct Tape Marketing,* **one huge factor contributing to the size of your marketing budget is the potential of each new client.** You should estimate how much revenue each client will produce over the course of two or three years. That number will provide parameters on your expenditures for the acquisition of new clients.

- ✓ Set revenue and new client goals
- ✓ Determine what a new client is worth to your business
- ✓ Calculate client acquisition cost
- ✓ Take your new client goal, multiply it by your acquisition costs, and you have your marketing budget

6

So, as Jantsch notes, if you would like to add 100 new clients next year, and a previous marketing expenditure of $5,000 yielded 12 clients, your marketing budget for this next year is $41,000 (or roughly the same $416 per new client you spent last year).

To sum it all up, as you prepare your budget, make sure to consider the following key components:

- ✓ Fixed annual expenses
- ✓ Consulting fees
- ✓ Web design
- ✓ Graphic design
- ✓ Printing
- ✓ Advertising
- ✓ Direct mail promotion
- ✓ Lead conversion

On average, small law firms typically spend about five percent of gross revenues on marketing and client development. In order of priority, here's a more detailed list of expenditure categories, as outlined in John Jantsch's book, *Duct Tape Marketing*:

1. **MARKETING CONSULTANT AND OUTSIDE ADVERTISING SERVICES**
   - Should you hire a marketing director?
   - Can you afford it?
   - If not, hire an assistant or marketing consultant
   - Hire an intern with enthusiasm

2. **ADVERTISING:**
   - **Network television**

☐ Mass Market Reach

☐ Most costly form of advertising

☐ Not suitable for small businesses

- **Cable television**

  ☐ More appropriate for targeting market niches or demographics

  ☐ You can now choose an industry-specific produced ad, customize it, and place a media buy-all in a matter of minutes www.spotrunner.com.

- **Radio**

  ☐ Less expensive, an effective technique for targeting potential clients, as long as you choose the appropriate channel (for example, a business program may be more fertile)

  ☐ Great for repetition of your message as listeners tend to be loyal

- **Local newspapers**

  ☐ Appropriate for retail enterprises

  ☐ Ineffective for most other forms of business due to a lack of targeting

- **Business newspapers**

  ☐ An efficient relatively inexpensive way to communicate with business-only markets

- **Magazines, cost variable**

- **Outdoor billboards**

  ☐ Very effective as a direct-response vehicle if your business is "location-based", but very expensive

- **Direct-mail**

  ☐ The best option for most small businesses as you

6

can purchase targeted mailing lists and fully control who receives your message

- **Telemarketing**
  - ☐ Almost completely ineffective
- **Internet**
  - ☐ Pay per click advertising sold based on clicks
  - ☐ Ads can be targeted to specific local terms and geographic location
- **Neighborhood flyer distribution**
- **Strategic partnerships** — collaborating with members of your law suite or a group of attorneys may be both economical and effective
- **Yellow Pages**
- **Social Media**
  - ☐ LinkedIn
    - ◆ Personalize your communication
    - ◆ Reach out to five new contacts per week
    - ◆ Find a genuine point of connection
    - ◆ Write personal messages that summarize your current work, what drew you to their profile.
    - ◆ Know when people view your profile
    - ◆ Build prospect list
    - ◆ Track job changes
  - ☐ Avvo (experienced lawyers on demand)
  - ☐ Facebook
    - ◆ Focus on the wall and newsfeed, adding content to your wall.
    - ◆ Share photos that encourage engagement
    - ◆ Build interest lists, topics that draw people in

- Create a public or private group with similar interests
- Advertise — you'll only be charged for the number of clicks or the number of impressions you've received.
  - ☐ Twitter
  - ☐ YouTube
  - ☐ Martindale.com
  - ☐ Bestlawyers.com
  - ☐ Lawyers.com
- **Firm brochure**
- **Client newsletter** (printing and postage) or E-newsletter Services, products, packages you offer
- **Office signage**
- **Production of community seminars and special events**

Miscellaneous:

- ✓ Sign up for Lawyer Referral Service
- ✓ Business entertainment
- ✓ Computer/library/publications
- ✓ Professional dues for trade and professional organizations
- ✓ Holiday cards and gifts/postage
- ✓ Referral gifts
  - A gift is a welcome surprise
  - A gift is tax deductible
  - A gift expresses interest and/or appreciation

- A gift is the essence of thoughtfulness, a personal touch
  - ☐ T-shirt, a coffee mug, a copy of your book, gift certificate

✓ **Postage**

✓ **Charitable contributions**

✓ **Club dues and expenses** (e.g., for Rotary club)

✓ **Retreats**

✓ **Stationery**

✓ **Extranets**

✓ **Intranets**

✓ **Client survey printing/postage**

✓ **Professional support staff training**

✓ **Have them take the Kolbe ATM Index/Instinct Test** (Kolbe.com)

Creating a budget can be one of the most intimidating actions to sit down and spend the time needed. Knowing this, we have created a spreadsheet template for you to use as you begin to project and create your budget.

To access this single most important tool when starting or revamping your practice, visit the Ironman resource page, www.PracticeLawLikeAnIronman.com/resources

33
Marketing Checklist Summary

When you utilize all these essentials of marketing, and have a budget to pay for them, you open up the door of your practice, allowing prospective clients to walk in.

To summarize, here are the six main components of marketing:

- ✓ **PRODUCT** (legal services)
- ✓ **PRICING** (hourly rate or flat fee)
- ✓ **PROMOTION** (sales, public relations, direct marketing and advertising)
- ✓ **POSITIONING** (astute choice of geographical location and online presence)
- ✓ **PEOPLE** (a staff that provides superior customer service)
- ✓ **BUDGET** (a percentage of your overall gross income to be determined)

Before launching your marketing plan, consider:

- What do you want the person who notices your marketing to actually do?
  - Call for an appointment
  - Send an email
  - Fill out a questionnaire

- **What do you need to build for this to happen?**
  - Website
  - Office intake system with answer scripts ready to go
- **How will you follow up to respond?**
- **How much can be automated through software like:**
  - Hatchbuck
  - Infusionsoft
  - Act-On
  - Wishpond
  - Ontraport
  - Marketo
  - Pardot
  - WordPress

And the foundation of it all is your **VISION STATEMENT**, previously discussed, one that summarizes how you want the world to see your firm.

- ✓ **What actions will you accomplish?**
- ✓ **What will be the practice's image?**
- ✓ **What in the local market might affect your future success?**

First and foremost, in whatever area of your specialty:

- **Be the best** in your area of practice, exhibiting expertise and high ethics.

- **Create an aura**, that story in marketing materials that projects your ideal image.

- **Network** intently, socializing, being available to all opportunities.

- **Create a sterling staff**, one that values superior customer service

  - Engage them in writing a summary of why your firm is unique.

  - Write a summary that paints a vivid picture of the ideal client.

  - Have employees adhere to brand standards in all communications.

  - Keep your staff in the loop, briefed on ads, mockups for direct mail pieces.

  - Make sure every employee realizes that their day-to-day performance influences the practice's overall success.

In the end, marketing is really all about creating innovative solutions, a social process that involves you, your co-workers, and clients.

✓ You must understand <u>your ideal client</u>, their personalities, desires, and behaviors.

✓ You must <u>differentiate yourself</u>, demonstrating how your services are superior to the competition's.

✓ And above all, you must <u>convey your unique skills and the perceived benefits of your practice.</u>

6

In marketing your practice, keep these fundamental questions in mind:

✓ Does your practice motivate and inspire clients?

✓ Can you innovate a marketing strategy that sets you apart from the competition?

✓ Can you infuse humor and personal connection into your business relationships?

✓ Can you link your practice to your community?

✓ Is your practice convenient?

- Are your contact details on every page of your website?
- Do you have outposts in social media sites?
- Do your search engine profiles contain key info?
- Do you offer multiple forms of contact (email, web form, click to call, IM)?
- Can prospects obtain additional information without picking up the phone?

✓ Does your practice exemplify a sense of efficiency?

✓ Do you offer clients the element of the unexpected?

- Unexpected gifts
- Handwritten notes

6

Remember, as John Jantsch points out in his book, *The Referral Engine: Teaching Your Business to Market Itself*, the 4 C's to success in your solo or small practice are:

- **CONTENT** (you're a lawyer so you have a sought-after skill to sell).

- **CONTACTS** (your ever-expanding network of clients and referrals).

- **CONNECTION** (your ability to communicate effectively in marketing).

- **COMMUNITY** (your integral relationship to your town and neighborhood).

In the end, if your branding is powerful and unique, a client will hire your firm, based upon these factors:

- Expertise and prior experience
- Cost
- Reputation
- Innovation, how you approach a matter
- Knowledge of the client's industry
- Personal chemistry

Ultimately, the client makes a predominantly emotional decision when hiring you. It's usually a gut reaction to the overall package of factors listed above.

I can tell you that in order to completely satisfy any client, you must understand their emotions and goals. Anticipating what they want, and how they think, has everything to do with the success of getting new clients, and referrals from existing ones. **Ask them:**

- ✓ What solution were they seeking when they hired you?
- ✓ What did you provide that they valued the most?
- ✓ What has been a result of working with you?
- ✓ What would they tell others who are considering hiring you?

6

To sum up the essence of all of this, I always refer back to one of my favorite books, John Jantsch's Duct Tape Marketing: The World's *Most Practical Small Business Marketing Guide.* In it, he discusses the

"Four Ps" of a fully alive business:

- ### PASSION

  - Good things happen when the founder of any business is driven by a personal passion — a compelling enthusiasm that drives you forward and fuels your dedication and caring. You feel as if THIS is the thing that you are meant to do. Your solo practice becomes the vehicle to serve others and produces the connections and income you need. Once you pinpoint your passion point, you need to connect it to a purpose.

- ### PURPOSE

  - "Purpose is how a business defines why it does what it does," notes Jantsch. This is your reason for being, the billboard that draws clients toward its doors, like a magnet. Purpose builds trust between its employees and customers and creates energy and enthusiasm. And that's why joining a purpose-filled business is like joining a cause. People will perform remarkably well when they're motivated in support of that cause.

- ### POSITIONING

  - You offer clients the core difference between you and your competitors. This is a promise of value to be delivered. You transmit the benefits your clients are going to get and use your niche as a positioning tool in the market. Consumers are always looking around for the best possible deal at the best quality and how these products or services will contribute to their success. The goal is that your clients become loyal ambassadors of your brand because you're offering them the expertise and attention they need.

■ PERSONALITY

- Your practice must capitalize on desirable personality traits to attract clients. It's one thing to state your purpose on a website or marketing brochure, but it's another thing to live by a tangible set of positive daily habits, language, and behaviors that offer proof of your purpose. Clients are drawn to people who provide clear, inspirational counsel. You have to be efficient, innovative, and sometimes even playful to create a fully alive business. These traits act as a filter for every decision made, how the business is run internally, and how the brand is experienced externally.

Don't forget to take full advantage of staff input to generate inventive ideas for marketing:

- Conduct short (15-20 minute) daily sales meetings with staff.
- Everyone should proactively act to help generate new revenues.
- It should include the following:
  - Setting revenue goals for the day, the week, the month, the year.
  - Pre-sales-call planning.
  - Cost-sharing sales tips and techniques.
  - Brainstorming, marketing hooks, promotions, and ideas.
    - ☐ **READING LIST:**
      - ◆ *How to Become a Rainmaker,* Jeffrey J. Fox
      - ◆ *Beyond Entrepreneurship,* James Collins
      - ◆ *Good to Great,* James Collins
      - ◆ *Scaling Up: How A Few Companies Make It… and Why the Rest Don't,* Verne Harnish

6

Finally, here's a valuable **checklist for creating and building your brand (your image and reputation),** based upon one of my favorite books, Jeffrey Gitomer's *Little Black Book of Connections: 6.5 Assets for Networking Your Way to Rich Relationships:*

- ✓ **Give to get** (provide complimentary consultations, at least to referred clients).
- ✓ **Think of your brand as a person, with a personality of its own.**
- ✓ **Don't attempt to mimic the look of chains or big brands.**
- ✓ **Generate community confidence by connecting in person.**
- ✓ **Establish yourself as a** (If permitted by your state):
  - Specialist
  - Leader
  - Innovator
  - Person who gets things done
- ✓ **Research what other law practices do to promote themselves**
  - What makes you remarkable?
  - How is your customer service different?
- ✓ **Be consistent, your brand carrying over into:**
  - Signage
  - Office décor
  - Voicemail message
  - Fax cover sheet
  - Office email signature
  - Stationery
  - Business cards

6

Questions To Answer

- ✓ How will your brand reveal your practice niche?
- ✓ What are your strengths and weaknesses?
- ✓ How will you set the standard for quality and inform employees and clients?
- ✓ How will you brand yourself as consistent?
- ✓ Consistency of message
- ✓ Quality and distinction of offering
- ✓ Inclusiveness of message
- ✓ What factors set you apart from the competition?
- ✓ How can you be the "go-to" lawyer in your community?
- ✓ Why should clients choose you instead of another practice in your community?
- ✓ What reputation have you earned to create your personal brand?
- ✓ What is your logo or tagline and what does it stand for?
- ✓ Does it reflect your personality?
- ✓ It should be a unique, powerful, memorable image.
- ✓ Use it on your letterhead, business cards, fax forms, firm brochures, invoices, and envelopes.
- ✓ How are you perceived in your community?

To access this interactive list and a full marketing summary, visit www.PracticeLawLikeAnIronman.com/resources

34
You're The Man! (or Woman!)

Beyond all these marketing principles, remember that **YOU** are your best advertisement. So wherever you go, be accessible, friendly, and ready to discuss your solo practice.

Have a 20-30 second elevator speech ready to use at any networking event. As John Jantsch explains in his book *Duct Tape Marketing,* this speech is your **TALKING LOGO, an extended slogan that conveys your area of specialty and unique ability.** It's a tool that allows you to convey the single greatest benefit of doing business with you.

- ✓ **Use a short statement that quickly expresses your firm's mission and compels a listener to want to know more**
- ✓ **First, address your target market**
- ✓ **Then zero in on a problem, frustration, or need expressed**
- ✓ **Next, prepare a simple supplementary answer that tells them the unique way you get them that benefit or solution**

As your marketing efforts unfold, in order to avoid feeling more in control and less overwhelmed, perform a **S.W.O.T. TEST, a diagnostic tool created in the 1960's by Albert S. Humphrey, an American consultant in management. It allows you to identify your:**

- **STRENGTHS**
  - What does your firm do better than anyone else?
  - Which firm qualities are most commonly praised by clients?
  - What makes you so successful?
  - Why do clients choose you?

- **WEAKNESSES**
  - In which areas do you wish you had more knowledge or experience?
  - What has caused you to lose business to the competition?
  - What aspects of your firm are you least likely to brag about?
  - What holds your firm back from being what it could be?

- **OPPORTUNITIES**
  - What are some things you wish your firm had time to do?
  - What trends could result in more business for your firm?
  - What impending changes in the law could affect your business?
  - What technological advances could change the way you do business?

- **THREATS**
  - What are the main obstacles to increased revenue?
  - Who is your competition and what are they doing differently?
  - How will impending law changes impact your firm in a negative way?
  - Do you have bad debt- or cash-flow problems?

Throughout the process of marketing and advertising your firm, you must become known as a **VALUED AUTHORITY** in your field.

6

CHECKLIST FOR BECOMING KNOWN AS A VALUED AUTHORITY

✓ Write an article or regular column. There are many opportunities:

- Print: magazines, newsletters, and journals, such as:
    - ☐ *Above The Law (ATL)-Small Law Firms*
    - ☐ *TYL (American Bar Association)*
    - ☐ *The Brief*
    - ☐ *The Champion (NACDL)*
    - ☐ *GPSolo*
    - ☐ *Human Rights*
    - ☐ *International Law News*
    - ☐ *Landslide*
    - ☐ *Litigation*
    - ☐ *Perspectives*
    - ☐ *Probate & Property*
    - ☐ *The SciTech Lawyer*
    - ☐ For more, check www.americanbar.org
- Websites, email newsletters, and blogs
    - ☐ Write succinct engaging articles and blog posts.
    - ☐ Use compelling stories told with style and good nature.
    - ☐ Check web-based publications such as:
        - ◆ GPSolo
        - ◆ eReport
        - ◆ Litigation News
        - ◆ Trends
        - ◆ Bar Leader
        - ◆ Consult: ABA Journal Blawg Directory
- Social media
    - ☐ Display your personality and test your traction.

□ Create a boundary between personal and professional posts.

□ Reposition: Use social media wisely.

□ **Use, "If This, Then That", or IFTTT.com.** This is a free web-based service that allows users to create chains of simple conditional statements, called "applets," which are triggered based on changes to other web services such as Gmail, Facebook, Instagram, and Pinterest. The program helps you automate tasks, providing shortcuts for tweeting and other social media postings.

□ **Use iMeet Central** (formerly Central Desktop), a Cloud-based software that allows you and your team to work on files, share knowledge, and manage your projects, including updates to company operations manual.

□ Also consider using **pbworks.com** and **sites.google.com**

✓ **Listserv:** Contributing to Listserv discussion is an effective way to get your name in front of other lawyers. The ABA's SoloSez is an excellent group discussion forum for solo and small firm lawyers.

✓ **Publish a book**

✓ **Speak at seminars in your practice field**

✓ **Speak at public community groups, such as the Rotary Club and Kiwanis Club**

✓ **Create a newsletter**

   • Attend a graphic design class at your local college and offer a reward for the best graphics.

✓ **Get involved and lead a community or civic group**

✓ **Take an active role in your trade or field of practice association**

✓ **Create a video for your website, YouTube**

✓ **Create a unique voicemail, fax cover sheet, business card**

35
Quick Final Review

No matter what vehicle you use for marketing, **content created for one venue can be reused for multiple purposes:**

- A tweet can be expanded into a blog
- A blog can be expanded into a published article or a newsletter
- An article can become part of an E-book
- A speech can be expanded into a seminar or a web conference.

Remember, **you can OUTSOURCE CONTENT** to a competent marketing firm, public relations firm, copywriter, or ghostwriter to write polished copy, or create content from scratch. All you need is a computer and you can easily interview and find the right people to help.

- Create a list of proposed subjects for blog posts or articles
- Using Zerys, InboundWriter, or Blog Mutt to identify potential writers
- Contract for a minimum of 12 blogs per month
- Even if you delegate, still create one post of your own each week

For marketing your firm, you should include:

- **Facebook**, featuring changing content, events, videos, announcements.
- **LinkedIn** profile updates.

- A **Twitter** account to engage followers with updated content.

- Active participation in **industry-specific social networking sites.**

- A **monthly newsletter** with fast reads and deep dives into key subjects.

- An **online web conference series** featuring industry-related guests.

- **Audio and video testimonials** from clients.

- **Articles** that can be contributed to practice-specific websites and publications.

- A **guest blog post** on high profile blogs.

- A series of **45-minute seminars** on trending practice-specific topics

- Uploaded images to **Flickr.**

- Client testimonial videos on **YouTube.**

For additional resources that will facilitate the planning of your practice as well as your implementation process, visit the Ironman Resource page, at
www.PracticeLawLikeAnIronman.com/resources

6

36
The Art of Networking and Building Referrals

"You can make more friends in two months by becoming interested in other people than you can in two years by trying to get other people interested in you."

-Dale Carnegie-

Now that you've solidified the branding and marketing of your solo or small practice, it's time to **master the art and science of NETWORKING.**

It's all about **proactively interacting with people** to expand your web of contacts. You convey authentic curiosity about their business and your desire to contribute to its success. That's what superstar networkers do: they add to the life and business of another person.

- **Great networkers are givers**
- **Great networkers are connectors**

They direct the focus onto you, not themselves.

That's why you're going to promote your law practice as a desirable and valuable entity not by "selling" it, but by developing relationships. Of course, we've spent pages on the necessity of marketing and advertising, which is hugely important, but never forget the human factor.

As **BOB BURG** writes in his fantastic book *Endless Referrals,*

"Great salespeople never push. They lead!" They also support, which is why networking involves helping others succeed in their lives and careers.

As I learned in one of my favorite books, *The Go-Giver* (by Bob Burg and John David Mann), the amount of money you make is directly proportional to the number of people you serve. It's caring about their needs and desires. So be a go-giver as opposed to a go-getter. **Give and you shall receive.**

In fact, the **rule of reciprocation** says that we as human beings naturally try to repay in kind what another person has provided us. That's the core philosophy involved.

Relationship building consists of:

- Reaching out to existing clients to strengthen existing relationships.
- Networking actively to meet potential new clients and referral contacts:
  - **Meet political leaders**. Back when I was in the prosecutor's office, I was able to network with many elected officials within the Greater Cincinnati community, which later helped me build my solo practice. You would be amazed at how accessible and receptive your district politicians will be, whether it's a city council member, judges, the elected county prosecutor, state senator, or U.S. congressman.
  - **Meet other lawyers**. I have also developed solid relationships with colleagues who refer me business.

- Meet commercial real estate salesmen/developers
- Meet accountants
- Meet bankers
- Meet insurance agents
- Meet a variety of business people

It's a process of getting to know people and engaging in relaxed conversation. You listen closely to what they say and show genuine interest in them. In the process, you put yourself in a position to exchange information and useful contacts.

The underlying subtext of all effective networking is the **ability to initiate, develop, and maintain relationships — building trust over** time. This is especially key in a solo or small practice law career.

According to the American Bar Association, as of 2015, there were **1,300,705** licensed lawyers in the U.S., so distinguishing yourself from the competition is crucial. After all, why should they hire you?

7

37
The Keys to Likeability

Beyond the obvious — your credentials and skills — I can tell you that **LIKEABILITY is one huge factor** in being retained as a lawyer. And it's an essential ingredient to networking. What is it?

Likeability is the ability to produce positive attitudes in others by increasing a sense of happiness and relaxation. According to a 2015 article in Forbes magazine[37], the keys to likeability:

- **Friendliness**—your ability to communicate openly with others.

- **Relevance**—your ability to connect with others' wants and needs.

- **Empathy**—your capacity to acknowledge other people's feelings.

- **Genuineness**—your integrity and authenticity.

- **Positive mental attitude**—you exude an optimistic vibe.

- **Secure**—being comfortable in your skin, no need to brag or talk incessantly.

- **Non-judgmental**—open to new ideas and ways of doing things

- **Vulnerability** — being self-effacing, admitting mistakes and difficult experiences.

---

[37] https://www.forbes.com/sites/travisbradberry/2015/01/27/13-habits-of-exceptionally-likeable-people/#4875c92a1b14

When you add it all together, that's a powerful prescription for success. In fact, according to the Gallup organization, **likeability is actually the #1 predictor for being hired** (or elected to public office). So when you're networking, remember that colleagues and potential clients are picking up on all the signals above.

Armed with these qualities, in the context of networking with potential clients, be prepared to answer questions like these:

- What do you see as most unique about your firm?
- Why did you start it?
- What advice would you give about starting out in your area of practice?
- What's the strangest or funniest thing you've seen happen in your business?
- What significant changes have you seen in your profession?
- What do you see as a coming trend in your area of practice?

And when you're networking, allow the other person to:

- ✓ Offer their perspective on the state of legal practice.
- ✓ Brag a little bit about their achievements.
- ✓ Talk about subjects that fascinate them — off the subject of the law.
- ✓ Share experiences that have been most meaningful in their lives.

Above all, in one way or another, you need to convey that your solo practice **CARES** passionately about the work it does—that it provides VIP service to every client, with impeccable representation and follow-up.

7

In order to transmit that message, you've got to expand your social outreach. So whether you do it over drinks, at lunches, conferences, and black-tie events, or at seminars, conferences, or workshops, **you've got to mingle.**

I can tell you that in a job market flooded with a wealth of legal talent, attorneys, and law students, you have no choice but to get out there. So be open and friendly. Be talkative and accessible. Use all your interpersonal skills. And start schmoozing!

The people best at this are **confident public speakers** and **attentive listeners.** Both qualities allow you to build rapport with a diverse set of people, putting them at ease and fostering trust.

In fact, establishing **TRUST is crucially important in attracting clientele.** While potential clients will assess your competence and track record, your **character counts** just as much.

REMEMBER: *People who know and trust you are your personal walking ambassadors. Help them help you! Make it easy for them. Train, teach, or brief those people in your inner circle about what kinds of cases you're looking for.*

7

38
Ice-Breaking
(Less Talking, More Listening)

Here are some TIPS to prepare you before any networking opportunity:

- ✓ Ice Breaking (Less talking, more listening)
- ✓ Eat beforehand to avoid struggling to eat and talk at the same time (and never talk with your mouth full).
- ✓ Don't lean on alcohol to calm your nerves. Play it safe with tea, coffee, water, or a soft drink.
- ✓ Introduce yourself with a firm but friendly handshake (DON'T go in for a killer grip!).
- ✓ Ask open-ended questions, which foster an atmosphere of congeniality and follow-up dialogue.
- ✓ Avoid interrupting.
- ✓ Do not overly talk about yourself [38]
    - But when you do, keep it brief.
    - Develop a short descriptive sentence of 10 to 30 seconds, describing what you do and how it could benefit the person you're talking to.
- ✓ Maintain eye contact (displays respect for the other person).

---

38 http://sfp.ucdavis.edu/files/163926.pdf
https://career.unca.edu/sites/default/files/15%20Second%20Pitch.pdf

- ✓ Utilize open rather than defensive body language, which builds rapport.

- ✓ Find common ground by asking feel-good questions, a technique described in the book, *Endless Referrals* by Bob Burg.

  - ☐ Use "FORM" questions

    - ◆ F=FAMILY
    - ◆ O=OCCUPATION
    - ◆ R=RECREATION
    - ◆ M=MESSAGE (what they deem important)

- ✓ Concentrate on giving, not getting (one of the principles outlined in John C. Maxwell's fantastic book *The 21 Irrefutable Laws of Leadership: Follow Them and People Will Follow You,* is that your influence is determined by how abundantly you place other people's interests first).

  - ☐ Ask questions about themselves and their business. In the book *Endless Referrals,* Bob Burg suggests these networking questions that work every time:

    - ◆ Tell me about how you got your start in the business?
    - ◆ What part of your work brings you the most fulfillment?
    - ◆ What distinguishes your firm from the competition?
    - ◆ What counsel would you give someone just starting in the business?
    - ◆ What do you observe as cutting edge trends in the law?

- What one phrase would describe the way you do business?
  - ☐ Express willingness to serve.
  - ☐ Pop back to talk to people again, leaving your business card.
  - ☐ Approach someone standing alone, introduce them to others.
  - ☐ Follow-up is everything:
    - Write a note (do not ask them for anything)
    - Give an appropriate gift — a book or CD
    - Send appropriate articles or newsletters that relate to them

Also suggested in an article titled: *The Art of Schmoozing: Networking Tips for Lawyers by Vault Law Editors:*

- Align yourself with more experienced practitioners.
- Gravitate toward the person who seems to be the center of influence in the room, the dominant force in a group of people chatting.
- Assert yourself in group conversations to broaden your exposure.
- To avoid feeling left out, arrive early and leave later, allowing increased chances to chat with panelists and others of interests.
- Avoid controversial or offensive topics
- Smile
- Be human (share a story or anecdote relevant to your life).

7

- End a conversation politely with an exchange of business cards — "Great talking with you, thank you for taking the time, let's connect soon."

Mental Preparation

✓ Determine your networking objectives

✓ Do your research on potential contacts to help guide conversations

✓ Prepare a short pitch of your strengths and goals for conversation

Appearance

✓ Be well-groomed.

✓ Match your dress code to the event (dressing up in a suit is always better than dressing down).

✓ Make sure you're comfortable in whatever you wear, as comfort boosts confidence. The focus should be on you, not your appearance.

As I learned in Jeffrey Gitomer's *The Little Black Book of Connections:*

The Secrets to Working a Room

- Develop your "30-second" introductory commercial:
  - Create a friendly introduction that engages the other person.
  - And/or probe to find something you have in common such as college, kids, sports teams, hometown.
  - What are their philosophies?
  - Establish a sense of expectation—that you look forward to continuing the dialogue at a future time.
  - Exchange business cards.

- Set up meeting time.
- Follow up with e-mail.

■ **Allocate your time wisely:**
- Spend 75 percent of time with people you don't know.

■ **Take advantage of the entire room:**
- Spend approximately 3 minutes with each person, that's potentially 20 contacts per hour.
- Let the size of the event dictate the amount of time you spend.

■ **Do not be pushy.**

■ **Do NOT try to "top them" (this is not a competition).**

■ **Do not beg for some sort of action or favor.**

■ **Ask questions to get to know the person.**

■ **Ask for their wisdom, advice, or experience.**

■ **Always connect with the HOST, and ask who attended and how to connect with them.**

■ **Exchange business cards.**

Remember These Networking Tips

✓ **Put away your phone and focus on the person in front of you.**

✓ **Make an effort to talk to trainees or support staff —you'll often acquire valuable insight and information from them.**

✓ **Avoid soliciting for a job; instead ask for advice.**

✓ **Present confident body language, a congenial facial expression.**

✓ **Always keep handy a small notebook, pen, and business cards.**

7

✓ Prepare ahead by researching people you most want to talk to.

✓ Follow up with them periodically but don't bombard them with emails or calls.

✓ Stay connected to friends you made at the university or law school.

✓ Never boast about your legal victories, instead listen more, talk less, allowing others the space to talk.

But no matter what you do when it comes to networking, the **#1 rule is that YOU MUST PUT YOURSELF OUT THERE.**

Networking is a contact sport.[39] It's like prospecting for oil. You've got to be in the field. So you must leave your office and connect with anyone and everyone in order to build up your referral network.

Sure, you may feel fearful or shy approaching complete strangers, but the more you do it, the easier it gets. And remember, you don't need to be naturally outspoken to be effective in networking environments.

- Be yourself
- Be open
- Share your experience
- Tell a funny story
- Demonstrate that you can deliver value when called upon
- Focus on the long term
- Don't get frustrated if networking doesn't yield immediate results

39 https://www.entrepreneur.com/article/249782

Once you make the initial connection, the conversation will flow. But don't expect instant results or miracles. Any business relationship has a rhythm to it. So be patient as the relationship unfolds.

In short, as cited in a 2014 Think It article titled, *7 Reasons Networking Can Be a Professional Development Boot Camp*, great networking includes:

- **Peer-learning**
  - Learn from others
  - Use the power of observation
  - Think of networking as a focus group
- **Always be ready**
  - Be quick on your feet when a networking opportunity appears
  - Be active and ready for engagement
  - Don't fall asleep at the wheel
- **Take notes**
  - Retention comes from taking down what you learn
- **Ask non-traditional questions**
  - Ask the unexpected
  - Reveal a personal story
- **Put your personal brand to the test**
  - Don't overly promote yourself
  - Talk about your enduring idea
  - Talk about what differentiates you from others
  - Whom you serve
- **Continue the conversation**
  - Invite a new contact to follow up with an email
  - A link to an article or white paper

- Reconnect at lunch or via LinkedIn, Twitter, Facebook
- **Hold yourself accountable**
  - Follow up! (By phone, email, social media messaging)[40]

While there is no substitute for in-person networking, **it can also be done by phone.**

When reaching out to potential clients: [41]

- **Prepare in advance (know who you're talking to).**
- **Begin with a compliment about their work**
- **Limit your own talking**
- **Focus on their needs**
- **Speak in terms of results**
- **Ask questions**
- **Don't interrupt**
- **Don't allow yourself to become irritated**
- **Listen between the lines**
- **Reflect back what you're hearing**
- **Hang up last**

In the end, building your practice is all about finding the right opportunities, and you never know what options a diverse network can yield. As Woody Allen once joked, 80 percent of success is just SHOWING UP. I think the percentage is obviously lower, as preparation and hard work are the real forces behind success. But yes, showing up is also key.

7

---

40 https://www.thinkitassociation.org/blog/june2012/7-reasons-networking-can-be-a-profession
al-development-boot-camp.aspx#.WO-o5FKZNJw
41 https://www.themuse.com/advice/your-6step-plan-for-a-perfect-networking-call

The goal here is to plant seeds that will eventually grow into long-lasting relationships. The person you meet at Friday's networking event probably will not help you on Saturday, but the interaction may lead to something substantial a year from now.

* * * * *

In order to deepen your existing network, keep these pointers in mind, as brilliantly summarized in Bob Burg's book *Endless Referrals*:

- **Start by brainstorming the contacts you already have**
  - This is your sphere of influence: people you know, who are already a part of your life (Every one of us has a **personal sphere of influence** of about 250 people)
    - ☐ Family
    - ☐ Friends
    - ☐ Casual acquaintances
    - ☐ Miscellaneous — mailman, plumber, tailor, haircutter, anyone who touches your life in some way
- **Contact your existing clients monthly**
- **Make a list of referral sources and contact them periodically**
- **Consider book clubs, running clubs, swimming clubs, cycling clubs, triathlon clubs, softball teams, and any group as a networking point**
- **Research, compile, contact a list of three logical targets weekly**
- **Make firm's capabilities known to friends, family, entire social circle**
- **Send clients, contacts, and referral sources articles of interest**
  - Send practical, educational information every four to six weeks

7

- Use electronic newsletters as a free or inexpensive yet powerful way to stay connected
- Focus on informing, educating, and adding value to your clients (do not turn this into a sales pitch)
- Use Constant Contact or MailChimp to manage your e-zine. It's free for up to 2,000 subscribers and up to 12,000 emails per month

- **Use your entertaining budget wisely**
  - Meals
  - Sporting or cultural events
  - Active interaction, games of racquetball, golf, or tennis
  - Firm retreats
- **Invite your client base to your speaking engagements**
- **Send notes of congratulations for accomplishments**
- **Send holiday and birthday cards**
- **Send thank-you notes or even a unique and thoughtful gift for referrals that helped you make a great fee**
- **Keep your mailing list fastidiously updated**
  - Never remove existing or prospective clients from your mailing list unless asked to do so
  - Remove all headers and footers so communications are personal
- **Track your results to identify your most and least productive prospects and referrals, then adjust your spending on those contacts accordingly**
- **Peer-to-peer education**
  - Current clients are best prepared to explain the value of your service to a prospect, including its limitations. Hold focus groups made up of several existing clients and several prospects

- **As recommended in John Jantsch's book, *The Referral Engine: Teaching Your Business To Market Itself*, create referral communities**
  - Put together a group of like-minded businesses, all focused on the same target audience, and then create a local online community, including a blog that each member of the referral group contributes to. This group could easily generate leads in a way that would allow everyone to win
- **Offer hospitality**
  - Allow community organizations to use your premises for PTA meetings, lunches, anniversaries, and charitable board meetings or even fundraisers

7

39

A Referral Engine Driven by Client Satisfaction

Everyone knows that REFERRALS are the most cost-effective marketing strategy out there. It's a mutual give-and-take that results in a win-win for everyone involved. It costs nothing to give or receive one. And the best source of referrals is a satisfied client. So every step of the way, you need to create a culture of client success and satisfaction.

> *Remember: People do business with those*
> *They KNOW, LIKE, and TRUST!*

Needless to say, a remarkable product (what you do) and the reputation you earn are the best ways to acquire new clients. That reputation builds a powerful referral engine, a subject brilliantly covered in John Jantsch's *The Referral Engine: Teaching Your Business to Market Itself.*

> *Remember, it's not just what you know or who you know.*
> *It's who knows YOU and what you do for a living.*

From my point of view, to make a referral engine operate, you must:

- ✓ Compile and create a master list
- ✓ Friends
- ✓ Business friends

✓ **Coworkers**

✓ **Important people with whom you're acquainted**

✓ **Christmas card list**

✓ **Relatives**

✓ **Members of organizations you belong to**

✓ **People you would like to connect with**

- Call or email

- Ask what their needs are for the year

- Provide valuable information

- Educate

- Send your core message

- Detail your full range of services

✓ **Remember the four things referral sources need to know**[42]

- Data to spot your ideal client, someone who fits the model perfectly.

- They must describe why anyone should work with YOU.

  ☐ This is your value proposition or "Why choose us?"

  ☐ Provide a suggested script that referral sources can use.

- They should know your follow-up process.

- They should know what's in it for them.

  ☐ Do not offer a monetary incentive for referrals.

  ☐ Reinforce the value for clients.

  ☐ Provide referrals back to them whenever you can.

7

---

42 http://www.therainmakerblog.com/2014/06/articles/law-firm-marketing/the-top-5-things-peo-ple-need-to-know-to-send-you-great-referrals/

✓ Tap into existing client connections

- Established clients are best prepared to explain the value of your service to a prospect.
- List the five most valuable clients with whom you work.
    - ☐ What was the result of your representation?
    - ☐ Did they become "raving fans?"
    - ☐ How have they helped you?
    - ☐ How would you like to help them in the future?
    - ☐ Contact those clients periodically.
- Time your request for referrals with the completion of a project well done.
- Suggest scheduling a focus group made up of several existing clients with new prospects.
- Conduct an annual Client Satisfaction Survey (ask clients what they liked most and least about your firm as well as what upcoming challenges you could assist them with).
- Compile a larger list of past clients and contact them periodically.
- Target three to five potential clients to whom you could sell firm services.
- List your three most valuable sources of referrals.
- Offer them a special report or "Top 10 Tips" sheet and request they update their contact information.
- Write out at least three reasons a prospective client should hire you (and include them in your marketing strategy).
- List one way you will thank each of them in the next thirty days.

✓ **Ask for introductions from colleagues and key business associates**

- <u>**Communicate the context**</u>—what kind of client you need and want.

- <u>**Guide them**</u>—pointing out successes they may not be aware of.

- <u>**Limit the requests**</u> —by not putting a burden on any one referral source.

- <u>**Shoot**</u> for once a week.

- <u>**Keep track of all contacts**</u> in a running log/customer relationship management system.

- <u>**Create an online community**</u> of like-minded practitioners, including a blog that each member of the referral group can tap in to:
  - ☐ Educate
  - ☐ Generate/share leads, which makes it a win-win

- <u>**Provide a script**</u>, a short pitch that summarizes your firm's expertise.

- <u>**Send**</u> a supply of business cards, pens, any portable marketing tools.

- <u>**Schedule**</u> a meeting.
  - ☐ Breakfast, lunch or dinner meetings.
  - ☐ Cocktails.
  - ☐ Golf, tennis, bridge, or theater.
    - ◆ What are your company's long-term business goals?
    - ◆ What are your personal career plans?
    - ◆ What are you looking for in a lawyer?
    - ◆ How can we be more valuable to you?
    - ◆ How often are you in a position to give referrals?

7

✓ **Acknowledge the effort**

- Send a personalized appreciation gift — a gift certificate, a gift basket, movie or sporting event tickets, a bottle of wine, etc. (if they put $10,000 into your pocket, a gift in the range of hundreds is appropriate).

- Include them on your holiday gift list.

- Create a referral news page on your website.

- Tweet the referral on your blog post, promoting their business.

✓ **Use technology (invaluable tips, as below, provided in John Jantsch's *The Referral Engine: Teaching Your Business to Market Itself*)**

- Read and comply with your state's code of professional responsibility when soliciting and advertising.

- Send a link to 10 referred leads inviting them to click or link for more information.

- The five who click get an automatic email message inviting them to attend a webinar next week.

- The five who did not click receive an email offering a free downloadable tip sheet.

- The five webinar invitees who did click are immediately followed up with your staff for phone contact information.

- If you're doing direct mail or web page marketing, are you following the response by using tracking codes?

- Are you creating custom fields in your prospect contact database or CRM software to note referral sources?

- Have you divided your clients into promoters, passives, and detractors?

- In your survey do you have a question like the following:

7

- How likely is it that you would recommend us to a friend or colleague?

- Are you asking your clients what you could do better and then fixing it?

- If you want to create or improve your referral numbers, go to **netpromoter.com.**

- **READ:** *Testify! How Remarkable Organizations Are Creating Customer Evangelists,* www.creatingcustomerevangelists.com.

✓ **Create strategic partnerships**

- Cultivate contacts with a varied cross-section of professionals in your geographical area to maximize opportunities:

  - ☐ Accountants
  - ☐ Attorneys in other law firms
  - ☐ Small business owners
  - ☐ Insurance brokers
  - ☐ Real estate brokers
  - ☐ Political representatives
  - ☐ Vendors

- Create value for partners, spreading the word about the excellence of their product or service.

- Touch people's lives and build networks

- To create effective partnerships:

  - ☐ Craft a letter of introduction defining your niche
  - ☐ Conduct video interviews
  - ☐ Host receptions for each referral source category
  - ☐ Express willingness to learn more about their business

7

     □ Consider co-branding, creating an information event about topics such as:

- ◆ Tax issues
- ◆ Marketing
- ◆ Human resources
- ◆ Buying and selling a house

- Create a landing page on your website that lists your strategic partners and what they offer.

✓ **Develop a client database**

- Buy a database of potential referral sources (www. infoUSA.com and www.superpages.com).

- Use a contact management system, such as:

  □ InfusionsoftforAttorneys.com

  □ Goldmine.com

  □ Salesforce.com

- Develop a top-ten desired-client list within each of your niche areas:

  □ Develop relationships with attorneys in your area of practice.

  □ Maintain option to do research/write briefs .

  □ If your calendar is too crowded, pass on that potential client to a colleague, an act of generosity that will reap returns.

  □ Take referring attorney to lunch, dinner, happy hour.

- Make an attempt to secure a meeting or, at least, a phone call.

- Perform research to develop a marketing plan for each potential client.

- Include law school alumni, high school alumni, church

members, civic organizations, philanthropic clubs, professional associations.

✓ **Expand client base with community involvement**

- Attend trade shows, continuing education, charities, professional organizations:
  - ☐ Rotary
  - ☐ Kiwanis
  - ☐ Lions
  - ☐ Chamber of Commerce
  - ☐ Jaycees (Junior Chamber of Commerce)
  - ☐ Places of worship
  - ☐ Local bar association
- Join the National Speakers Association and attend their convention.

✓ **Define your differentiators**

- Focus on your competitive advantage by answering this question: **Why should someone hire me versus any of my competitors?**
- Focus on the **benefits**, **value**, and **results**:
  - ☐ Get clients/associates to review YOU on social media.
  - ☐ Become a local phenomenon (press interviews/ coverage).
  - ☐ Emphasize the VIP treatment your staff provides.
  - ☐ Prove your firm's excellence by blogging
- Create a form letter that includes who you work with, how you are different, and a personal invitation to get together.

7

☐ Focus on solutions (People don't buy legal services, they buy solutions to their legal problems).

☐ Prepare a case study of how you found a creative solution to another client's problem.

- Send out 10-20 letters per week:
  - ☐ Your firm's profile
  - ☐ Newsletter
  - ☐ Business card
- Have your assistant follow up with calls, appointments for lunch or coffee.

✓ **Create a Business Advisory Group:**

- Your lawyer (business lawyer)
- Your accountant
- Your banker
- Your financial planner:
  - ☐ Invite them out for a meal or event.
  - ☐ Schedule a formal sit down meeting with them twice a year. Meet with each one of your advisory group members individually 3 to 4 times a year.

7

40
The Five Reasons Why Lawyers Don't Get Referrals[43]

- **You believe that your education and background is enough, that referrals will magically appear on their own.**
- **Working with your office staff was a negative experience:**
  - Did the client have an extraordinary experience being attended to by your team? Or just an experience?
  - Did you treat your client with extraordinary customer service?
  - Did you host networking events?
  - Do you have www.JS-KIT.com, which is a collaboration tool that allows prospects to rate and review your practice.
  - Did you capture customer success stories and testimonials on video?
  - Was your staff happy to see the client?
  - Did the staff follow up the visit with a phone call?
  - Did your staff survey the client for feedback?
  - Did your office look clean and organized?
  - Did your staff reach out to your clients regularly?
  - Did you acknowledge the birthday/anniversary dates for clients?

---

43 *Renegade Lawyer Marketing: What Today's Solo and Small Firm Lawyers Do to Survive* and *Thrive in a World of Marketing Vultures, 800-Pound Gorillas and LegalZoom,* by Benjamin W. Glass

- **Making referrals to your office had mixed results:**
  - A client may feel trepidation in making a referral due to past history.
  - Did it take you too long to return phone calls?
  - Were you late for meetings?
  - Did you send the client paperwork in a delayed time frame?
  - Were your documents full of errors?
- **You didn't adequately THANK your referral source:**
  - Did you pick up your phone and thank the referral source?
  - Did you write a personal thank-you note?
  - Did you send them a small gift for thinking of you?
  - Did you acknowledge them in a newsletter or blog?
  - You never gave back:
    - ☐ You have to practice the "give to get" rule, providing referrals and benefits of your own to sources.

So don't forget to:

- **Join an association that supports your practice specialty.**
- **Speak when you can on your area of expertise.**
- **Attend conferences/seminars/trade shows in your area of expertise.**
- **Work on a 30-second infomercial about the firm.**
- **List qualities of your practice that differentiates it from the competition.**
- **Let people know the full range of legal services you provide in your practice.**

7

41
Mentorships Count!

As we've seen, as a solo or small firm practitioner, you're the boss, ultimately responsible for all hiring and firing. As we've seen in all the pages preceding, you're the CEO of your firm, wearing many hats in order to establish yourself.

And just as your employees will frequently come to you for direction and advice, you likewise will want your own source of guidance and counsel. We've already talked quite a bit about your peer group and circle of influence.

But, as we draw to a close, I want to re-emphasize the **importance of having a MENTOR (or more than one!).**

As we've seen, as a solo or small firm practitioner, you're the boss, ultimately responsible for all hiring and firing. You are also the firm's director of human resources, attending to the ongoing challenge of staff support and mentorship.

And just as your employees will frequently come to you for direction and advice, you likewise will want your own source of guidance and counsel. We've already talked quite a bit about your peer group and circle of influence.

For this relationship to work, personal chemistry is key, a compatible personality match that encourages a close, candid bond between mentor and mentee.

After all, your benefactor is going to be your most trusted guide and your role model, someone you can observe and turn to for advice as needed. And one day, of course, you will return the favor and pay it forward, and become a mentor to someone yourself.

All in all, as summarized in a Leadership Resources online article, a great mentor will be:

- **Available:** By phone or email or in person to share a meal or golf game, etc., to build the relationship.
- **Patient:** We all process advice and information at different speeds.
- **Sensitive:** Tact and diplomacy are crucial in addressing your fears and weaknesses.
- **Respectful:** Knowing when not to push too hard is critical.
- **Flexible:** You can't control anyone or anything and must shift and adapt with the flow.
- **Supportive:** He or she should express pride for what the mentee has accomplished.
- **Knowledgeable:** Mine the mentor's area of greatest expertise.
- **Confident:** A mentor is self-assured.
- **Non-competitive:** Not threatened by your success.
- **Encouraging:** Providing a support net during tough times.
- **A good listener:** Being a sounding board can be as valuable as giving any one piece of advice.
- **Concerned:** Able to express a genuine sense of caring.

When you sum it all up, the role of a mentor is epitomized by the acronym BEST, as defined in John Maxwell's book *Mentoring 101*:

- **B: Believe**
- **E: Encourage**
- **S: Share**
- **T: Trust**

A Mentor...

✓ **LEADS BY EXAMPLE,** as a positive role model, allowing you to model their ethics, values and standards.

✓ **SHARES LAW PRACTICE PROCESSES** — knowledge of court culture, procedures, office staffing, and overall philosophy.

✓ **CELEBRATES YOUR ACHIEVEMENTS,** is never threatened by your success.

✓ **MOTIVATES YOU** to establish goals and reach your potential.

✓ **KNOWS WHEN TO WAIT** before giving advice.

✓ **ASKS THE RIGHT QUESTIONS,** reading your body language and state of mind.

✓ Is **OPEN-MINDED** and controls their own emotions.

✓ Is **FORTHCOMING** about their own mistakes.

✓ **EXPOSES YOU TO OUTSIDE ACTIVITIES:** continuing education, classes or projects, books, events, people, etc., to hone your skills and foster networking.

✓ **ENHANCES** your confidence and self-esteem.

✓ **PROVIDES GUIDANCE UNCONDITIONALLY,** with no expectation of payback.

7

With mentors who can do all this, you're going to prevail over any solo practice challenge that comes your way.

You're now armed with multiple checklists that will allow you to:

- ✓ Maintain your entrepreneurial mindset
- ✓ Visualize your law practice as you want it to be
- ✓ Create a hyper-efficient office with automatic systems
- ✓ Hire and nurture an office team with the right stuff
- ✓ Brand and market your practice to separate yourself from the herd
- ✓ Network your way to new connections and fulfilling relationships
- ✓ Master client services and fees

With all that, you're on the pathway to success as a valuable practitioner in your community. Remember: Yours is an Ironman practice, strong, dedicated, disciplined, educated, inventive, and brave. Such qualities can only lead to your ultimate victory.

For additional resources visit the Ironman Resource page at www.PracticeLawLikeAnIronman.com/resources

7

EPILOGUE

Epilogue

Now that we've come to the end of the book, I want to **THANK EACH OF YOU** for joining me on this journey. I understand how taxing it can be to launch a solo or small law practice.

As we've seen, the intricacies of setting up a law office are time-consuming and complex. And to do it successfully, you need an abundance of physical and mental energy.

And that's why I want to leave you with a final remembrance of my experience as an Ironman.

As I mentioned from the start, it was my experience as a four-time Ironman competitor that welded into me the values and standards that changed my life.

It was all about:

- ✓ <u>Organization</u>
- ✓ <u>Training</u>
- ✓ <u>Determination</u>
- ✓ <u>Discipline</u>
- ✓ <u>Dedication</u>

These were the traits that encompassed everything I ever did.

EPILOGUE

I remember that at the start of my first Ironman, during the ocean swim, there were 1,600 participants crowded around me. Before the race began, we all waded over thirty minutes in the ocean. I had to struggle and fight my way forward, with competitors jabbing and kicking me with the same goal.

Just before the starting gun went off, I felt a big ball of anxiety, all that nervousness creeping in. Still, I had the absolute conviction that I could finish the race. My only fear was that I might get injured along the way.

In the months leading up to the competition, I had to lose weight and assiduously train my mind and muscles for speed and endurance. Everything had to be tightly scheduled, including my regimen of weightlifting workouts, stretching, and massages. I had to work smartly and efficiently.

Likewise, as we've seen, you need to plan every aspect of your law practice too. You put your regimen on a calendar and execute the given game plan every single day.

I also learned that I performed better as an Ironman when I sought out help from others. That's why I worked with a coach, rather than only reading training books.

I did the same thing later in life, when I turned to legal coaches, the mentors who helped me launch my solo law career. This, as we discussed, is your Mastermind Alliance, a group of people who can offer a gold mine of knowledge, experience, and inspiration.

From that **MASTERMIND ALLIANCE,** I learned the critical skill of **delegation** and how to expand my practice while pacing myself. Otherwise, just as in Ironman, I'd burn out without getting to the finish line.

The good news is that I always reached that finish line, but not without extreme physical discomfort and intermittent doubt.

But once I was actually at Ironman for the first, second, third, and fourth time, whenever I felt pain or when exhaustion overwhelmed me, I had a mantra:

"I'm feeling smooth, I'm feeling good, I'm having the greatest race in my life ... I'm feeling smooth, I'm feeling good, I'm having the greatest race in my life ..."
over and over again.

And it worked. This was the effectiveness of positive thinking, a vital aspect to creating a solo practice as well. Your mind is powerful. And you can nourish it with either positive or negative thoughts. And that's why, earlier in the book, we talked about incorporating a mantra into your routine when you're feeling fear, pain, or pressure.

You sit down and mentally rehearse what you have to do in order to succeed. And when negative thoughts begin to creep in, you have to stomp them out with positive thinking.

By doing this, you're fighting against fear by dancing with it, rather than allowing it to overwhelm or conquer you.

By using a mantra during the first stage of my first Ironman, I was able to settle down and get into my flow, a groove that allowed me to succeed.

 When I finally emerged from the ocean (feeling elated!) and went on to the brutal 112-mile bike ride, I faced the formidable hills and head-and-cross winds of Hawaii.

I was always careful to use brand new tires to help me stay ahead of the Ironman cycling pack; many of my competitors got flat tires along the way. (Likewise, in your practice, you should always use cutting-edge equipment where possible.)

As for those headwinds, from long experience, I can tell you that, as a lawyer, there are days you'll be facing brutal head-and-cross winds too. You'll be pushing and grinding away, even though you don't seem to be getting anywhere. But you must press on. **YOU MUST ENDURE THE EXERTION. You must follow your training methods and keep cranking away in those tough situations.** Trust me, you will get through it. Just keep your mind focused on the end goal.

That's what I did at Ironman. When that segment came to an end, I jumped off my bike, briskly put on my running shoes, and began the marathon.

Now you endure the heat and the pain. Fatigue is creeping its way in. The adrenaline high fluctuates. This is where you really have to pace yourself and visualize feeling cool, though it's hotter than hell. You take it one mile at a time.

My friends, that's exactly how you need to think about your law practice. It's a twist-and-turn journey, and a long one. It takes time to train and to compete at a high level. You must be organized and execute the game plan. Just as I did, you need to dig deep down and focus on the finish line. That takes a lot of the pain and fear away.

In the end, you WILL get to the finish line. You will create a thriving practice.

And to get there, my final advice is to practice law like an Ironman, and not just in the courtroom.

Be an Ironman in your marketing, with your clients, your staff, and with those you choose to network with. Practicing that way, you will be unstoppable.

So here's to a happy and successful practice.

Aloha!

E

E

As a special bonus, I have compiled a comprehensive reading list of all of the books I have read over the years. These books contribute to many aspects of my success, both in my own practice, and also in writing this book. This list can now be yours if you log on to the Ironman resource page at www.PracticeLawLikeAnIronman.com/resources.

65920956R00188

Made in the USA
San Bernardino, CA
06 January 2018